*For Paul and Jasmine, who listened to my
ramblings, held my hand, and waited patiently
while I made sense of everything.*

IV

THE RALLYING CRY

HEALING THE HARDEST PARTS OF LIFE THROUGH CREATIVITY

SUZIE JAY GOLDSMITH

CONTENTS

INTRODUCTION 1

THE END OF THE BEGINNING 7

CHAPTER ONE: CREATIVE SELF-CARE 23

CHAPTER TWO: LETTING CURIOSITY LEAD 51

CHAPTER THREE: THE MINDFUL PHOTOGRAPHER 71

CHAPTER FOUR: WHOLEHEARTED CREATIVITY 99

CHAPTER FIVE: PER ASPERA AD ASTRA 127

CONCLUSION 151

WORKBOOK: THE PRACTICAL "HOW TO" BIT 157

TRIGGER WARNING

While it is my hope that this book be helpful, it would have been impossible to write without including some of my personal experiences of TFMR.

A border has been added around particularly triggering parts, should you wish to skip them for now. For those whose grief and trauma is still raw and fresh, these pages will be here for you to turn back to, whenever you're ready.

"When you tell the truth, your story changes.
When your story changes, your life is transformed."

Mark Matousek

INTRODUCTION

If you knew something bad would happen tomorrow to change the course of your life completely, how would you react? If you were to go to bed, then wake up and live that awful day you knew was coming, would that make you brave? Or just human, and unable to prevent the things that sometimes befall us.

When I first had the idea to write this book, I had several motivations in mind. In an ideal world, I want to be heard. And I can't fully explain why. Even if no one reads this though, there are things I need to get off my chest, if only to lighten the load. To draw back the curtains and let the light in.

I'd also like to shine a little light on the TFMR (Termination for Medical Reasons) warriors. The women who take the pain so their babies don't have to. The ones who've held my hand as I've wept for my own, so very wanted, so very missed. A community shrouded in shame and secrecy for fear of misrepresentation, the ones who give me courage to air my wounds so that they might heal.

The closest most parents get to the world of TFMR are the scary leaflets delivered a few weeks prior to the first prenatal ultrasound at 12 weeks. Screenings for syndromes like Down's, Turner's and Edward's; life-limiting medical conditions, anomalies and various abnormalities so rare and terrifying they don't even have a name yet. For most people, it's a brief glimpse at a life they could never recognise as their own. A mere flash before their eyes and then it's gone. On to happier times, on to the birth of their babies.

And yet for some of us, there's a bullet in the barrel. The force of which will change your life forever. Many choose not to speak of their experiences. It's not for me to comment on the individual reasons people keep their stories close to their chest but would it shock you to know that there are lots of us out there? Squirrelled away from the pro-lifers, too broken to stand up and declare that yes, we too value life. People may judge, but they'll never know the depths of love we feel for our babes.

> *"I've never been in greater pain than I am right now. And what I've learned about pain is that it's not to be numbed, it's not to be ignored and it's not to be wasted. And I'm going to use every bit of this pain, as fuel." - Glennon Doyle*

I wanted to share this quote early on to let you know that this book isn't intended to be a one woman pity party. This isn't a story of remembrance for my babies who've gone on ahead. This book is a rallying cry for the grief-stricken, the ones who struggle to feel OK with the way life's turning out. It's a chance for me to wave my flag of hope and put into words that not only is it possible to feel human again after devastating loss, but that it's actually possible to become the very best version of yourself, and thrive.

Of course I've worried that these words might be too specific to be helpful, the experiences of which I'm speaking too rare to be relatable. But as I stare at the planning post-it notes on the back of my kitchen door, amongst the inspirational quotes and the stories, I see the universal truth staring back at me. That grief, in all its forms, is inevitable and unavoidable. The sooner we dare to name it, the sooner we can begin to make sense of it. Grief for loved ones lost, for the ending of chapters, collective grief during a global pandemic. The loss of our freedoms and grief for the person you once were when carefree was all you knew. Whatever your hurt, consider this book your permission slip to grieve.

And let's not forget the emotional challenges of parenting after loss. Whatever our story, we're all just wavering somewhere along the anxiety line. Watching our children sleep and feeling the pang of protective love. Those mama bear instincts rise to the surface as we catch our breath at how beautiful yet vulnerable they look, wanting to protect them at all costs.

Night-time is for yearning but during the day, chaos sweeps us up and you know as well as I do that it's hard to love all the parts of parenting, as much as we wish we could. My hope in writing this book is that I can share the things that I find helpful on my emotionally complicated journey and that even if it's only in a very small way, they might be helpful to you too. They say that books often land in the hands of people who need to read them and I love that idea. So here it is, the book I wrote for you and I.

Introduction

THE END OF THE BEGINNING

24ᵀᴴ DECEMBER 2018

I'm inclined to believe that the universe has a bit of a twisted sense of humour. There I was on my daughter's second birthday, Christmas Eve, holding a Mr Tumble cake and singing "Happy Birthday" just days after my second TFMR (Termination for Medical Reasons). As if that wasn't surreal and difficult enough, I'd just contracted a ridiculously painful and debilitating strain of Hand, Foot and Mouth disease, the effects of which would stretch on for months. Apparently, only 1% of those infected get it so bad that all their fingernails and toenails fall out. So I guess I must be super duper special to once again be in that teeny tiny category where I've told myself *that'll never happen to me* and have it happen anyway. Odds mean little to me these days. I've been the unlucky 1 in 4, the 1 in 150, the 1 in 4000 and wishing it weren't so never made a blind bit of difference.

But to cleanse myself of the end I need to go back to the

start, to retrace my steps and slowly peel back the hurt. This is where creativity comes in.

Once upon a time, a couple in their thirties fell pregnant. After a previous miscarriage they'd made it to the 12 week mark and began to relax. They started sharing the happy news with family and friends, excitedly planning for the future. She knew in her heart it was a little boy. A sweet gentle soul, she thought. Toying with a growing list of names proved a welcome distraction from the morning sickness, which lasted all day, by the way. On her better days she put on music and danced. With her hands on her belly she connected with the life inside, already recognising herself as a mum. Recognising herself in so many new ways. That woman was me.

We sailed through our 12 week scan on an easy breeze. The only thing of note was that the baby looked a little "lazy". With nervous, self-deprecating humour, I jumped at the chance to remark that he must take after me. Tapping into the narrative of my childhood and school reports that always seemed to read "could try harder". *Oh yes, that explains it*, I thought. *He definitely takes after me.* I leaned in to take a closer look at the screen, pausing to observe that he looked like a tiny alien. Skeletal. Two dark pools where his eyes should've been. All appeared well though. He shuffled and wriggled on queue with no cause for concern. We skipped out of the hospital and made the happiest calls of our lives to loved ones. Everything looked A-Ok.

The weeks that followed were the culmination of plans where everything happily goes your way. Time off work and a road trip to Aberdovey, Wales to visit one of my childhood hangouts. My partner Paul and I had booked a room with a view of the yawning estuary and life slowed as we set our days to the ebb and flow of the tide. Life was good. My appetite was back, so we indulged in gluttonous breakfasts followed by fish and chips on the beach. One morning when the tide was high, we took ourselves off to the pier for a spot of crabbing. Piercing pink meat onto pristine hooks, we dangled our lines lower and lower into the dark below. A satisfying thump on the seabed and it's time to simply sit back and wait. The trick to crabbing is patience. Patience and good bait. Every now and then you give a gentle *tug-tug* on the line and hope to feel the extra weight of a crab or two. Most of the time, as you hoist your bounty, the weight gets lighter and lighter. A frustrating indication that one by one, your catch is dropping off along the way. Those savvy little critters. More often than not, all that emerges from the water is a salty wet stump of flesh, the good bits torn off by ruthless claws. But every now and then, with enough gentle motion, it's possible to pull your line and keep pulling, to go all the way, and be rewarded with a lovely little crab.

The sea was generous that morning and we caught plenty. I turned each crab upside down for my own little gender-reveal amusement. Pyramid line for a male, dome shape for a female. We plopped each one into water-filled buckets, listening to the soft scrape of their claws as they tap-danced on the sides. Later we released our catch on the beach and watched them race back to the waves. I took photos, as is usual for me, but there was one big difference. One huge fact that framed my days: we were officially going to be parents.

Summer came and went, and with the arrival of autumn, our 20 week scan. Paul smiled and squeezed my hand as we sat in the hospital waiting room. A sickly sweet smell hung in the air as other people's kids clambered over the chairs around us. Time ticked over. Pregnant couples filed in and out, giddy with glee upon exit. Every now and then the water cooler belched into action, my stomach flipping along with it. The nerves bubbled up, but don't they for everyone? And then we were called.

We saw the baby moving straight away. Palpable relief. Then the room fell quiet. Deafening silence as we waited for a reassurance that would never come. I breathed deep and tried to relax. Lying back, I traced my fingers along the edges of the bed, cold hard metal bringing little comfort. The ultrasound technician spoke at last, asking "Have you been leaking fluid lately?" I racked my brains. *Had I? No...Maybe?..Not sure.* I panicked. Was I already failing as a mum in missing something that could be so vital? *I didn't think so, no, definitely not.* More silence. So very little said in that room. The clock ticked on. I looked at Paul and Paul looked at me, as if pooling our confusion might add up to some kind of understanding. It didn't.

Eventually, the ultrasound technician spoke again. He explained that there was no fluid around the baby and they needed to work out why. The lack of fluid also made it hard to see anything in detail. We needed more tests but there were no appointments until the following week and we'd have to travel to a different hospital, in Central London. With wobbly knees and a gut full of dread we had no choice but to make our way home and wait for the next seven days. *Well it couldn't be that bad if they're sending us home, right?* We pacified our worries with reason. Looking back, I half-wonder if the technician quietly closed the door on us and thought to himself, *well, they're f****d.*

The wait that week was agony. Dr. Google did his worst as I ventured online and explored the possibilities ranging from treatable to fatal. I convinced myself that no fluid was somehow my fault. I must've done something to cause this. I took punitive measures to make amends and did the only thing I could naively think to do. I started drinking copious amounts of water. Obsessively so. *If the baby needs fluid, then fluid it shall have!* That week, I drank more water than is humanly possible. I'm talking gallons. I lived on soups and fruit salads, all washed down with yet more H_2O. There were target-setting charts on the fridge and everything. I tried in vain to turn myself into a human fish tank so my baby could have all the fluid he needed. To grow and splash about like Esther Williams on a good day. I don't know about you, but when things start to unravel in my life, I have a tendency to grapple and grasp. I get busy. I become manic in the face of fear in an effort to soothe my anxiety, stress and other uncomfortable feelings. An assertion of control in order to feel in control. When it comes to the creation of life though, there really is no control.

The day of the follow-up scan finally arrived. Central London. Big boy machines and high ceilings. "I've been drinking lots of water!" I beamed to a blank-faced ultrasound technician. Warm jelly oozed once more and she waggled her wand into action, deftly guiding it this way and that across my abdomen. With one glance at the screen it was clear to me that there would be no magic moment, no great reveal. I could tell that all that effort hadn't made a blind bit of difference. Positive thinking had failed me. There were questions met with more questions. Vague statements of what they could and couldn't see followed by feeble smiles. And yet more silence. "I just need to talk to my colleague," said the sonographer, and off she went.

I once saw a clip taken moments before the Indian Ocean tsunami hit Thailand on Boxing Day 2004[1]. Human life dotted the shore as the water stretched away from them. Looking out to sea, people seemed to marvel at the wonder of nature, full of awe and dark curiosity. Knowing the outcome, I watch that clip through gritted teeth, willing them to move away, to run, to try to save themselves. But the water was coming regardless. So relentlessly powerful it would flatten the land, destroying everything in its path. It would come and keep coming. Things would get much worse before they would get better. Efforts to run and hide would be pointless. No house would be high enough, no door strong enough to keep the water out. Futility in the face of such force.

My own tsunami was on its way. The water would come and keep coming. As I sat on the edge of the bed, kicking my heels and twiddling my thumbs, I waited patiently for the door to open again. I felt unsure of what was coming but sensed in my heart that it probably wasn't good.

There's no easy way to tell you about this next part, no way to sugar-coat the truth. A new woman entered the room and introduced herself as a senior consultant of fetal medicine and in a very matter-of-fact way told us that it was not a case of *if* our baby would die, but *when*.

I can picture that room, that moment, down to the very last detail. I'm transported back there every now and then at the most inconvenient of times, such is the nature of trauma. It felt unreal, staged almost. Unrehearsed and unprepared. The ridiculous moment of the pie in the face. The woman in the white coat said her lines and at first, I said nothing. What she said went something like this:

"Your baby has no kidneys and when the kidneys don't develop they can't produce amniotic fluid and without amniotic fluid your baby's lungs can't develop so he (you knew it was a boy right?) has zero chance of survival you know if one kidney had developed we could've explored the possibility of a transplant at birth but bi-lateral renal agenesis is a fatal condition so you have two choices you can either carry on to term which I wouldn't recommend because if he lives that long it will be incredibly traumatic for yourselves and awful for the midwives who would have to deliver your dying baby who will likely only live for a few minutes or you can terminate the pregnancy and we can make arrangements for you to deliver in a few days obviously you'll need some time to think about this but first let's move you to another room where you'll be more comfortable…"

An ocean of disbelief stretched out to the four corners of the room. It spilt over window ledges and under the door. Suffocatingly calm and black as it continued to fill the room. I went to speak but nothing came out. The hollow of my mouth belied the horror that lay there. The words that should've been on the tip of my tongue sought solace down the back of my throat, gagging me until they eventually erupted in a guttural noise. Shock pressed down on my airways as I felt a thousand things and nothing all at once. Numb with inadequate emotion.

The doctor seemed surprised by our reactions. I think she thought we knew. She seemed to be there on the understanding that her role was merely to provide a second opinion, to confirm what we already knew. But we didn't know. So here she was delivering the news that my womb was essentially a ticking time bomb. That a condition completely incompatible with life and the very worst of Dr. Google's prognoses, would ultimately take our little boy from us.

At the time, I inwardly directed my rage at her. I was so angered by the way she told us. Her manner seemed so cold and detached but now, on reflection, I think I get it. I recently heard Dr. Brenda Kelly, another senior FMU consultant speak of what it feels like to deliver this kind of news to parents. She explained that she was the police officer, pushing open the rusty gate to knock on someone's door at 3am. There to deliver the very worst news of someone's life. And how it feels to do this job hasn't diminished one little bit in her twenty years of doing it[2]. Maybe a little detachment is the only way.

Just when I wanted her to stop talking, just when I needed to hide and make it all go away, she told us that decisions needed to be made. When people talk about the initial responsibilities of parenting, they generally mean making sure your children are fed, clean and happy on a daily basis. Our first responsibilities as parents lay in deciding how our boy would die.

We were promptly bundled off into a different room to discuss our options which can be summed up as bleak and yet more bleak. A sterile white room with a squeaky sofa and a sad box of tissues close by. From a place of selfish horror, my mind was then flooded with the double-whammy of stark realities, as the water kept coming and coming. Not only was our baby going to die, but my first and possibly only experience of giving birth would be that of death. There was no other way around it, they said. I was too far along and out of alternatives.

Giving birth to death really affects a person, you know. Never mind the fact that this is your own flesh and blood, the one you're meant to protect. I said it over and over to myself until the ugly truth sank into my bones: *I would have to give birth to a dead or dying baby*. It all just felt so incredibly impossible.

So, what would a termination at 23 weeks entail? I asked the question then kind of wished I hadn't. First, a lethal injection through my abdomen. Two inches down and one to the left of my belly button. A needle to his heart. Painless and quick, they promised. Then home. A tiny corpse floating inside me for two days before I'd be able to deliver. As brutal as that might seem, it's actually not uncommon to have a delay between the feticide (awful, awful word, I know) and delivery. Each time I tried to imagine how it would go my brain seemed to shut down. Some things really are just too impossible to imagine.

Paul and I left the hospital needing time to think, time to talk. The Tube ride home *(why, oh why did we choose to take the tube?!)* was surreal. I sheepishly covered my "Baby on board" badge, feeling like a fraud, hoping no one would offer me a seat. I glanced over to a man completing the Metro crossword, his weathered hands scrawling their way across the tiny boxes. No word of a lie, two of the choices from our baby names list were written there. Oscar down, Leo across. Suddenly it no longer felt right to use any of the names we'd pondered. This was not the motherhood I had envisaged for myself. Was this even motherhood? Parenting such as this surely needed a new name. He needed a new name.

It was so hard to know what to do with ourselves when we finally made it home. We sat on the sofa and stared at the wall for a while, eerie quiet lapping over us. Brief respite. It felt such a relief just to be home and make the world stop for a moment. I'm not even sure how long we stayed there like that, wordless, motionless.

Sometime later that day I reached out to a friend who told me about a charity, Antenatal Results & Choices (ARC). I'd never heard of them before. In case you're unfamiliar too, ARC is a national charity that helps parents and healthcare professionals through antenatal screening and its consequences. Although they are non-directive, they are the only UK organisation offering specialised bereavement support for those who end a pregnancy after a prenatal diagnosis. I should add that due to working in this sensitive area of family life, they find it incredibly difficult to attract funding[3]. We've since raised money for them and donate when we can, as do many other TFMR parents. I hope they will always be able to continue their essential work. Without ARC, I don't know quite what I would've done.

I called the helpline and spoke to one of the loveliest women in the world, Sally. She spoke slowly and gently. She held space for my confusion, panic, fear and despair. She agreed that it was all so incredibly unfair. Sally didn't try to fix anything, how could she? But she did suggest that I start writing. She said that if I felt comfortable, I could write letters to my baby, that the process might help. I'll admit I was a little dubious at first but desperate for some sort of outlet. As soon as I put pen to paper the words poured out of me, along with the tears.

As I wrote to my boy, an image of Charlie Brown came into my head. The little boy with the sweet gentle soul, slightly tinged with sadness. I'd loved the *Peanuts*[4] cartoons growing up and it felt like the perfect name for our little boy. So there it was, Charlie.

My letters to Charlie came thick and fast. Sometimes sad, sometimes joyful. A strange and painful mix of grief and gratitude. It might seem odd that I would mention gratitude this early on but in spite of everything, I really was grateful for him. I cherished every kick and squirm, along with the chance to be his mum. I felt thankful that his movements had finally become strong enough even for his dad to feel. Sleep eluded me during that time and I think those hours spent writing at 4am laid the foundations for what could only be described as some sort of spiritual awakening.

I wrote for many weeks until the hurt began to subside. I wrote until I fell pregnant again. Anyone who finds themselves pregnant after loss will vouch for how psychologically complicated it can be. During your lost pregnancy, your entire belief system collapses. All the things you know to be true no longer apply.[5] With a subsequent pregnancy, you go from thinking *nothing will go wrong* to *everything could go wrong*. It's only natural to feel this way and well-wishers telling you to relax and stop worrying only seems to make things worse. Keep calm and carry on isn't quite so easy anymore. When I fell pregnant again in 2016, six months after my first TFMR, I did my best to bunker down and focus on the day to day. Part of that meant putting aside my letters to Charlie. After a stressful pregnancy which was thankfully straightforward, our beautiful rainbow baby, Jasmine, was born.

Fast forward to 2018 and the time came to try again in the hope of completing our family and provide a living sibling for our little girl. Two pink lines and the journey began once more. I plodded through first trimester fatigue and faced the sickness with as much stoicism as I could muster. I tried my best to push the worries and anxiety away and focus only on each day, each tiny milestone. I comforted myself with the fruit and veg comparisons of our growing bean. Strawberry one week, plum the next. Harmless, light-hearted distraction. But at the end of 2018 I found myself back in the unthinkable, against the odds, facing my second TFMR.

Those far wiser have taught me that it's never a good idea to share the things we haven't fully processed yet, so this is all the detail I'm really able to give about this particular part of my life right now. I will however, share more of Charlie later. What I can say about my most recent TFMR is that the grief has felt so very different. I'm learning to cope with loss all over again. The footprints in the snow have vanished and I still can't quite find the way back to myself. But I'm going to keep trying, determined not to lose my heart in the mess of it all.

Repeated trauma and loss over such a short space of time has taught me that there are no experts in grief. That every experience can be powerful enough to knock you off your feet. I'm not ashamed to admit that I struggled to pick myself up this time. It's felt more like a dragging of bones and muscle as I slowly hunch and inch my way towards the light. And yet I'm determined not to be beaten by life's cruel blows. Determined to honour my babies through my efforts to hold my head up and live life to the fullest. For them, for myself, and for my living little girl, who needs me.

"There is a vast difference between positive thinking and existential courage." - Barbara Ehrenreich

Chapter One

CREATIVE SELF-CARE

I watched a *Netflix* documentary a few months ago called *The Creative Brain*. There was one part in particular that I found fascinating. A veteran soldier named Ehren Tool had returned from the Gulf War. He was deeply shaken by what he had seen and found his experiences incredibly difficult to deal with. Unsure what his next move should be, he let his curiosity lead him to, of all things, a pottery class. He began creating ceramics that addressed the uncomfortable themes of trauma and loss. To his surprise, his works were incredibly well received and he now boasts a thriving business from his creative work. Ehren noted that the most common reaction from people was one of connection and meaning. His work enabled him to channel his feelings, start a conversation and feel connected[1].

With a similar tale, *Disney* animator Floyd Norman,

after being drafted to active duty, said he found drawing to be a great way of coping. In his words: "I was able to get through this traumatic experience by drawing cartoons."[2]

Then there is Elle Wright, author of *Ask Me His Name* who speaks of her house renovation project following the death of her son, Teddy. Writing of her home, Elle uses the kind of language that brings to mind a sacred space of salvation: "I have poured my heart, soul and every ounce of creativity into these walls. It's a sanctuary in more ways than I could even put into words...I truly believe that it is this house that enabled me to start to let the light in again. It gave me the courage to start to try to be myself again, it wrapped itself around me when I needed it the most and gave me a place to focus my mind".[3]

Whether it's home-renovation, baking, writing, drawing, singing, dancing, photography, knitting, flower-arranging, hand-lettering or any number of alternatives, creative self-care is up for grabs and available to all. Soothing our souls with the task of making something. It's powerful stuff. And at a time where many of us are reaching for ways to nurture our emotional and psychological well-being, I think we could all benefit from a sprinkling of what author Elizabeth Gilbert rightly calls "Big Magic".[4]

THE BEAUTIFUL ESCAPE

After my most recent TFMR at the end of 2018, we made it through Christmas and limped our way into the new year. In an ideal world, I would've hidden away until I felt a little better. As a toddler mum though, I had no choice but to keep going. The inexorable march of life threatened to squash me into the ground if I didn't at least try to keep up. In my mind, I just had to get up every day and put my best foot forward. What I found most tricky was that I had no space to deal with my feelings, to process the really difficult experiences I'd just been through. My sweet little girl still needed all the snacks, all the time. She still needed me to be all things for her. Not being able to give her the best of myself only seemed to add to my feelings of worthlessness. It's really hard to explain to a two year old that you just need a minute or two.

So I threw myself into something, anything, and began cleaning incessantly. Immersing myself in a physical task gave my mind room to breathe. The scrubbing and de-cluttering offered a welcome distraction from the chaos of my thoughts. While I sometimes lack the discipline to sit alone with my emotions, a good old scrub can be surprisingly meditative. It took me out of my head. The mindfulness of task definitely helped but eventually, I needed more expression. The cleaning fell away as I began taking more photos than usual. My photography style began to shift to reflect my mood. Shooting light and bright no longer interested me. I sought comfort in long, dark, winding shadows. I began to capture silhouettes that hinted of a life imagined. I read a lot and started writing again. These daily efforts lit a fire under me. I felt inspired and alive. My emotions purged, my soul cleansed, a little bit, day by day. Creativity quickly emerged as the most useful and effective way to feel better.

"Art is the only way to run away without leaving home." - Twyla Tharp

If you've ever played an instrument or sung a song, you'll know that when you're immersed in that task, there really is little room to think about anything too big. Less space for overwhelming negative thoughts or feelings. In that moment, all you have to do is get to the end of the song. For a few minutes, it's that simple, just get to the end of the song. It's quite the relief for busy, anxious minds.

How many of us relegate creativity to the bottom of the list? Self-care limping somewhere nearby? We're often so busy with life that we forget to do the things that nourish our spirit. And yet studies show that maternal depression often peaks at four years postpartum.[5] That's too many of us struggling for far too long to keep those embers burning. Creativity probably isn't even on the radar for some, too quickly dismissed as unproductive, self-indulgent or just a plain old waste of time. But if we aren't creating, surely we're just consuming. Turning up and tuning in to whatever it is we're to be sold that day. Gobbling up someone else's ideals on how life should look. But perhaps a happy life isn't something that can be achieved via external means. Maybe it's of our own creation. And what if it's entirely our responsibility to strive for it? What if deep, lasting joy and contentment lies within us and the simple act of making things, every day, is where it starts?

I try to imagine each day, responsibilities and all, as a blank page to be filled. When I try to fill that page with things that make my heart feel big instead of small, it becomes easier to focus on the now, to live in the moment. Laments of the past and worries for the future fade away, with less time available to dwell on them. When the future feels big, scary and uncertain it feels comforting to bring the focus back to one day at a time. Each day is ours for the making and in my experience, thinking this way somehow brings calm to an otherwise emotionally chaotic existence. Creativity can be our greatest ally during hard times. It's breathing-room for the brain. A welcome distraction as well as an expressive outlet. It can help us make sense of the madness. I'm willing to concede that for many, the creative path might, at first glance, seem like just another chore. It's why it's often overlooked. But creativity gives us back so much more than it asks of us. The return on a modest investment is huge.

> *"I think I need to keep being creative, not to prove anything but because it makes me happy just to do it...I think trying to be creative, keeping busy, has a lot to do with keeping you alive." - Willie Nelson*

Doing something creative can be as simple or elaborate as we choose. For me, I like to keep it simple. I keep my camera on the side and my lenses in the fruit bowl. For it to work, I need creativity to be easy and accessible. One of the things that puts me off going to the gym is the time it'll take to get changed, walk to the gym, do the exercise, then shower, change and walk home. Just thinking about it all puts me off! I know I'll be rewarded from the effort but in all honesty, time spent on things that aren't directly linked to the feel good buzz frustrates me. Being pretty time-poor, I love that no quicker than I've had the thought, I can get going with something creative. It's a much more efficient way to access my self-care. Within minutes I can be feeling lighter than I did before.

As a typical mum juggling parenting and work, it's tricky to sit down to a big creative project. For me, creative self-care is a series of small efforts that when added up amount to something worthwhile. A daily practice, if you will. Gentle and inoffensive. I squeeze it in whenever I can. It seems to work best when I can weave it around my parenting responsibilities and working life. This might mean setting up a simple a play activity for my daughter, Jasmine, in a pocket of light, near a window. When she comes to investigate, I have my camera to hand. Big camera or iPhone, it doesn't matter. Her play will be interspersed with moments of my joining in and moments where I sit back, observe and quietly photograph. Those points in the day are amongst my favourites. Something for her, something for me. It feels like the best kind of collaboration.

I take my camera along on our mornings out. The woods, the playground and the streets to wherever we are going are filled with opportunity and the chance to sneak a little creativity in. I should add that I always try to be mindful of her mood and won't press on if I sense she's not OK with being photographed that day. It's a delicate dance and one I hope we'll be able to continue for many years. With this in mind, it feels important to respect her feelings around it. The plants, the birds and the light however, are always obliging subjects.

I keep notebooks dotted around our home for writing. I thrash out lines in the notes section of my phone. Again, this isn't something I sit down to for hours on end. It's stolen moments, but so worthwhile. In the words of freelance writer Laura Pashby, "I'm addicted to the moment of bright clarity when sentences come together to tell a truth, to the satisfaction of having poured something of myself onto the page".[6] Yep that's it exactly. And the funny thing about writing, and all kinds of creativity for that matter, the more we exercise that muscle, the stronger it becomes. When we embrace creativity little and often, we are rewarded exponentially. Words that feel stuck begin to flow a little easier. And who wouldn't wish for an abundance of *flow* in their life?

I also play ukulele. The adult equivalent of the recorder. Super cheap and easy to learn. Teeny tiny and cute enough to be left out all the time. I pick it up for 10 minutes here and there. Jasmine's entering a *Disney* phase now and that works for me. All the lessons are sitting on the Internet waiting for me to tap into them for free. Do you see what I'm getting at? It's little and often. Jumping head first into those tiny pockets of time when they present themselves. It takes tuning in with a keen eye to begin to spot them.

I'll be the first to admit that living a creative life isn't always easy to achieve. I have days when making time and space for the things that make a difference in my life feels easier than others. The imperfect balance of work, motherhood and self-care takes constant tweaking and practice. But through the mindfulness of task and the feeling of accomplishment, herein lies my happy place.

In case you're not yet familiar with "Maslow's Hierarchy of Needs", allow me to throw a little light on the subject. According to a psychological theory developed by Abraham Maslow in 1943, human beings have five different categories of needs. Maslow assigned these five needs to hierarchical levels within a pyramid.

Those lower down, towards the bottom of the pyramid, can be categorised as basic or material needs. These include essentials such as food, water, rest, safety, security and so on. Understandably, in every life, these needs must be tended to first. When these basic needs are met, we begin to rise up the pyramid, next addressing psychological or spiritual needs such as love, friendship and feelings of accomplishment and respect. At the very top of the pyramid lies the area with the greatest potential for growth or *self-actualisation*. This area refers to our feelings of fulfilment, living up to our potential and becoming who we really are. Self-actualisation will look different for everyone, but it is interesting to note that creativity, spontaneity and problem-solving reside in this zone.[7]

MASLOW'S HIERARCHY OF NEEDS

SELF-ACTUALISATION
Creativity, Spontaneity,
Problem-Solving

ESTEEM
Confidence,
Achievement, Respect

LOVE/BELONGING
Friendship, Family, Intimacy

SAFETY
Safety, Security, Good Health

PHYSIOLOGICAL
Food, Water, Rest

In choosing a triangle or pyramid shape to depict his theory, Maslow implies a certain structural truth of human existence. Although we can't live on spirituality alone, it surely can't be right to only focus on the material either. As I understand it, when we strive to complete the pyramid shape in our own lives, making sure each category of needs is met from bottom to top, we begin to feel whole. Finding this out was something of an "Aha!" moment for me.

GIVE YOURSELF PERMISSION

Have you ever stood at the sink and felt the weight of the grind bear down on you? I know I have. Even without the added challenges of prior pregnancy loss, parenting is tough. Not all parts of it are fun. Some parts are incredibly challenging and some parts are just plain old duty-bound.

We don't address the endless list of daily tasks and chores because it's fun, we do it because we love our children and want the very best for them. But what if we could do the best for them, while at the same time, the best for ourselves too? This is where creative self-care comes in, healthy habits of self-expression, something small every day. It's of course tempting to ask *how can I possibly fit this in on top of everything else?* But what I'm learning is that making time for creativity can feel energising rather than overwhelming. And it's possible to fit it in where at first it might seem impossible.

Imagine a jar of stones. Big, bulky stones all the way up to the top. At first glance the jar appears full, no room for anything else. But find a few smaller stones and it's possible to fill the gaps as they rattle and scoot their way to the bottom. Now the jar is full. *Or is it?* Take a bag of sand and begin pouring the sand into that jar. Watch as it trickles and snakes its way through the cracks, filling every nook and cranny. Finally the jar is full, the jar is whole. We could view our days in much the same way. We could look at those big, weighty stones that take up so much space and think that there's no room for anything else. But if we're smart about it, there's actually plenty of time to be had and we don't even really need to take anything out of the jar to make it fit. It's not so much about filling each day to bursting point, but finding opportunities to do the things that we always say we'd love to do *if only we had the time*. If we make time for these things, a little each day, we don't necessarily feel more tired for having tended to them. I know that when I make time for the things that light me up, I feel energised, rather than tired.

Viewing our days this way isn't about being as productive as possible, packing in as much as we can. It's not about filling to the point where each day feels *full*, but filling to the point where we feel *whole*. Everyone's jar will look different. It's about finding time for the things that nourish our spirit, seeing opportunities where before it might have seemed as though there were none.

As I mentioned earlier, the easiest way for me to sneak creativity into my days is to do it alongside my parenting duties. I'm best able to do this through photography. The digital age gets a bad rap with naysayers accusing us of missing the moment, lost in technology, not being present, in order to take a photograph. But I would have to say that, for me, the opposite is in fact true. That having my camera to hand actually helps me *better* connect to the moment as I notice all the little details so that I might photograph them. It grounds me to the now. The light, the composition, the story. The nuances of my daughter's character that I'm sometimes only able to really see and appreciate after I've caught them on camera.

They say that the days are long but the years are short. And it sure is a bittersweet passage of time. As parents, we long to be present and soak it all up but with a moment of honesty, let's concede that a child's world isn't always the most mentally stimulating for us grown-ups. I feel OK admitting that. I don't think it makes me bad or ungrateful. Don't get me wrong, I love to get down on the floor and play with Jasmine. I love to chat to her and see things through her eyes. I wrap my arms around her often. Playing with her is a huge part of my life, but after hosting the hundredth tea party, my enthusiasm starts to wane. I'm only human after all. So I love working creativity into my days wherever I can. It feels good to wake up my brain in that way.

We don't really find time, we make time. Writing, for example, often seems to come in moments. On the London Underground I carry a notebook and scribble things down for later, grabbing that tiger by its tail before it's gone. Smartphone notes are just as handy. Going with the flow rather than waiting for the perfect moment is how inspiration invites us in. The more we accept the invitation, the easier it gets.

To label something as a *practice*, means that it's something we work at every day. It's never quite perfect but we do our best to try today, and then again tomorrow, and then the next day, and the next day. If we fall off the wagon, rather than giving up, we can simply try again. It's a continual process of imperfect effort, rather than expecting to arrive at a single point and be done.

I've developed a creative practice that feels right for me. I create things every day for the simple reason that it makes me feel better to do so. Sometimes my efforts will be big and sometimes tiny but always, something. When I'm really pushed for time, it might be as little as arranging the food on my daughter's lunch plate in some way. Nothing Pinterest-worthy, just a simple shuffle of pleasing shapes. Sparking my brain with the basic question of *what can I make with what I've got?* It might seem banal but to see beyond that, what we make hardly matters. It's more about the process, and what that brings to our days, than the end result.

Weaving a daily creative practice into my everyday life started with the smallest efforts, hardly anything at all really. But the more I flexed that muscle, the stronger it became. As time went on I felt so energised by these little acts of making that before long, I became a little greedy for the buzz. I've come to love the way I feel when I use my brain to make something that wasn't there before. It lifts me in a way that feels good for me and therefore good for those around me. So these days

I like to take a little more time for it. This inevitably means taking one or two of those stones out of the jar. If I want to simply do a little ukulele-playing or photo-making, write a poem here or there, I can definitely just use the tiny pockets of time that already exist, as long as I know where to look. But to catch a bigger fish, like writing this book for example, I've needed more time. I've had to learn how and when to take that time and the biggest thing, without a doubt, has been giving myself permission to do so.

"Mothers are the members of society who need to be given the most permission to be able to do the things that ignite their own souls because there's some deep, deep sense in the world that once you are a mother, your life belongs exclusively, entirely and only to your children." - Elizabeth Gilbert

When I was knee-deep in my post-TFMR cleaning phase I also became a little obsessed with healthy eating. I took pride in finding new recipes online and cooking everything from scratch. Although this was time-consuming I didn't really mind. It felt like a good way to distract myself during the evenings that threatened to stretch out and consume me in negative thinking. Simple, gentle creativity. One of my favourite weekly rituals was making homemade granola. It might seem insignificant but I loved that little task. The crunch of the seed and the smell of the baked honey. It was healthy but so incredibly tasty. Knowing that we'd all eat it (my fussy eater included) and that it would also add nutritional value to our days made me feel, well, a little bit smug. I liked feeling smug about my granola. But as self-expression became a growing presence in my days, I began to realise that I couldn't possibly do it all. As time management expert David Allen notes, "you can do anything, but not everything."[8]

I could have thrown in the towel right there and admitted defeat. I could have believed that living the kind of creative life I had set my sights on just wouldn't be compatible with my reality. I could have believed that I didn't have a choice. Then it dawned on me. I didn't have to make the granola. I could buy it ready-made from the supermarket and still be a good mum. I could also save myself a good hour or two a week of faffery. That time saved could be used somewhere else, on something that would light me up from a place deep inside. I could use the time to create something that would fill me up a lot more than granola.

From a position of first world privilege I can say, hand on heart, there is usually a choice. The choice may not be favourable, but it exists nonetheless. We *can* choose, it's simply the consequences that are out of our control. Telling ourselves it's not possible to take a camera with us to the park because we've got too much to carry, for example. Well the truth is, we do have that choice. We could choose to take the camera. The consequence of that might mean that our back aches a little more at the end of the walk. Maybe that's a consequence we prefer to avoid and that's fair enough. But the choice remains.

I think that living creatively is about mindset more than anything. You could say that you don't have time to write that short story you've had in your head for a while now, but what if you just started writing, in any small way, during whatever time you have to yourself. The consequence of this might be that you have less time for *Netflix* or social media scrolling and maybe you're not quite ready to give that up just yet. My only point is that although we might not like the consequences, there is usually a way to opt-in if we want it enough.

So I guess I've had to get quiet with myself and work out my list of non-negotiables. The things I have to/ want to do, no matter what. Client work and keeping my daughter fed, well and happy are top of my list of priorities. Beyond that, pretty much everything is up for grabs in terms of time. I shave off a few evenings a week of TV time, I do less cleaning (!) I only use social media when I have something specific I want to do there. I try to allocate my life minutes with intention. If I feel like resting, I can choose that too but I try not to do it every evening out of habit or boredom. This kind of intentional living feels right for me, putting my best foot forward for a life well-lived. It helps me feel like I'm regaining a little day-to-day control in a world that seems determined to keep throwing chaos and hard times my way.

BARRIERS

In her *Magic Lessons* podcast, Elizabeth Gilbert spoke to Erin, a mother of two young children aged six and nine. After years of blogging, Erin had a book idea that kept gnawing at her, wanting out. She talked about a guilt that she felt for having a passion other than looking after her children. She feared it would take her focus away from family life. The crazy thing was that Erin's kids were now in school. Every day between the hours of 9am-3pm she had time available to her and yet every time she sat down to write, procrastination would show up to stop her in her tracks. Luckily Erin had the superpower of self-awareness. Every week, she would get very quiet with herself and eventually realised that her procrastination was really something else.[9]

Procrastination wears many masks, sometimes guilt, sometimes fear, sometimes something else altogether. For me, with my own writing, it's fear. Fear that I'm not clever enough or eloquent enough. Fear that I'm too lazy to reach the end of a project, so why bother? But I'm learning the value of simply *doing*. The power of just getting stuck in and figuring things out as I go. We don't advance our skills or work out our creative direction by thinking; it takes action to move forward and improve.

It's about taking that first step and then the next, only looking as far as the one right in front of us, as the path begins to clear. And the path only really becomes visible when we look back, in retrospect.

The phrase "start before you're ready" is fast becoming a mantra of mine and every time I feel tempted to procrastinate and put off writing, I know it's not because I don't want to do it, but because I'm doubting myself. Procrastination is really just fear in sheep's clothing. So I'm learning that the trick is to simply notice the resistance and thank it for stopping by. Then gently move it away so I can get back to my task. It's a case of feeling the fear and doing it anyway.

Every day my brain tries to ask me the same thing: *who the hell are you to be writing a book?!* But we can rewire our thinking by just starting something and doing it a little each day in spite of those nagging thoughts. It seems to me that the best kind of growth usually happens somewhere outside of our comfort zones. So these days, if something feels bigger than me, I try to take that as a good sign that I'm on the right track.

Honestly, simply taking action in spite of what our brains tell us is so, so powerful. Besides, we shouldn't always trust our brains. After all, they are not always very capable of sensing the difference between a physical threat and an emotional one. The fight or flight response can be as powerful during a moment of failure or rejection as it is when we are faced with a snarling dog. I've noticed that with writing, as with most things, the more we practise, the easier it comes. So delve into the thoughts and memories that move you. Use them and your voice will amplify over time.

My partner Paul is a venerable creative with many years design experience under his belt. I think one of the reasons we get on so well is that we love talking about what it means to live a creative life. He feels the same as I do about the benefits that creativity can bring, maybe even more so. He's busy making things even when he's not busy with client work.

A busy day for me is, I'm sure, much like your own. I'll tend to client work, show up on social media, deal with my inbox, do all the usual mum and house-running duties. Busy, busy, busy, and my creative self-care has unintentionally been relegated to the end of the day. I'm down to my energy reserve tank and running on empty. On days such as this, where I'm shattered but recognise the benefits of doing something energising, I rely on the litmus test that Paul and I like to call the "ten minute trick". It's a very straightforward motivation hack. It's simply facing the reluctance and saying to yourself: *If I can just do ten minutes....*

When I try this approach and give my task just ten minutes of my time, more often than not I'll end up staying for longer. I've tricked my brain into starting and now I'm here I don't want to leave. After all, this is the thing that nourishes my spirit. Or, if I find after my ten minutes is up, I really don't want to carry on, then fair enough. I can still feel a little buzz of accomplishment that I gave it a go. *Well done me.* Win, win either way. The "ten minute trick" is about recognising that sometimes there's more at play than simply being tired. There can be hidden barriers to our creativity that stop us from pursuing our interests. For me, procrastination is sneaky fear and that fear of failure can show up as resistance. It would stop me doing many things if I let it. Of course sometimes, not wanting to create might genuinely be because you're tired. And that's OK. If you need rest, then go rest, friends. Just choose one or the other, with intention.

When feeling long-term resistance for a creative project, I find it helpful to pause for a moment and think about why that might be. Journaling these thoughts can help. We can always hide behind the busy work of motherhood and general life stuff and say that we don't have the time but as mentioned earlier, I really think it's about choice. Choosing a tiny, creative act of rebellion in a world where the alternative is simply doing what we need to get by.

With the right approach, a smattering of creativity can be easily achieved. A few doodles or sketches here and there, a dance in the kitchen, no problem. But a meatier project takes a little more thought. I can only really dedicate a few uninterrupted hours a week to writing the larger parts of this book and it can be hard. But I really feel that when I make creativity one of my non-negotiables, life becomes a little bit more exciting. I really need that for myself right now (and I bet secretly you do too).

With a meatier project in mind, it doesn't have to be a drag. With limited time at your disposal, you have to get creative not only with the task itself, but with how you find time to fit it in. The way I see it, this is just part of the challenge and working out this problem has the potential to feel just as exhilarating. There's a certain freedom that comes with limitations. Creativity can be the thing you sneak off in the night for, making you feel ten years younger. It makes you feel alive in a way that is completely unique. It's yours and yours alone, unless you choose to share it with the world.

> *"Telling yourself you have all the time in the world, all the money in the world, all the colours in the palette, anything you want - that just kills creativity." - Jack White*

Constraints on our time can be an asset. I have to say, I feel more decisive and creative as a busy, plate-spinning mum than I ever did as a singleton, running my first photography business from my home with endless hours stretched out before me. Limits on my time encourage me to be intentional and specific as to how I want to spend the precious life minutes I have available to me.

For the past six months or so, Jasmine has been having a "Daddy day" every Saturday or Sunday. This was born from a burning desire to get to my creative work in a way that the gaps in the week just wouldn't allow. Not being able to get to it for any great length of time was bringing me down. Weekends used to be 100% family time, all three of us. In taking a Saturday or Sunday morning for myself, where Paul would take Jasmine out, I initially felt incredibly guilty. I also felt incredibly ungrateful.

I'd wanted to be a mum above everything else. It took thousands of hours of morning sickness, hundreds of hours in hospitals, two labours and one funeral to finally get to a point where I could hold a living child in my arms. I'd worked harder to make that happen than at anything else in my life. I'd swallowed the trauma and anxiety to try again and again when every fibre of my being wanted me to run the other way. I'd gone through all this to become a mum and here I was asking for time off? No, that didn't sit well with me at all. But we tried it out anyway. And I saw how happy Jasmine was to be able to spend some one-on-one time with her dad. I saw how their relationship, completely separate to me, blossomed and flourished. I also noticed the difference in myself. The chance to honour my creativity brought me joy. It made me feel lighter and more content to be able to be at my creative best. So I gave myself permission to continue.

Owning our realities with compassion means that we can take a moment to reflect on our specific life circumstances and ask ourselves: *what would I be willing to compromise in order to follow my heart?*

Negotiating time for creative self-care doesn't have to be to the detriment of our children's well-being. With a moment to reflect, there are several unexpected positives as I've come to believe that pursuing our own interests is good for our children. For starters, I don't think it's all that healthy for our families to have all of our attention, all of the time.

Julia Cameron, in her book *The Artist's Way for Parents* describes how, as a single mother, she had to support herself and her young daughter through her writing. She couldn't afford not to write so she very quickly learned how to do so with a toddler crawling at her feet. Setting a clear boundary with the words "mommy's writing" taught her daughter valuable autonomy. She notes: "Domenica did not resent me writing. In fact, before long, she began to write herself. As the years passed, the toy horses gave way to journals. She wrote poetry, short stories, brief plays- the very things I had been writing as she played with her golden palomino at my feet."[10]

When children have the chance to get bored every

now and then, there is opportunity to discover and nurture their own creativity. They need those gaps in our attention to be able to do this. The possibilities that arise from letting our little ones explore the boundaries of their boredom is no bad thing. It's fertile ground for the imaginations of fire-breathing dragons and twinkle-toed ballerinas.

I think it's also important to remember that our children are watching us. How we lead our own lives and the choices we make matter. If we model martyrdom they will likely grow up to be martyrs. When Julia Cameron modelled creativity for her daughter, she grew to be a creator.

Writer Cheryl Strayed talks openly of taking herself off for three weeks in order to finish the first draft of *Wild*. Her children were four and five but as she put it, leaving the family domicile felt essential in order to immerse herself emotionally, spiritually and intellectually into her memoir, just to get it over the finish line. She felt guilty about leaving but within ten minutes of returning home, it was as though she had never been away. Her children were fine but more importantly, she had shown them what drive and dedication looked like.[11]

> *"One of the greatest gifts I have given my children is the example of a mother who pursues her passions like a motherf****r." - Cheryl Strayed*

So if there's something you're itching to try, please give yourself permission. Joy is infectious. When our children see that there is something in our life that lights us up, they reap the benefits in more ways than one. I believe that creative self-care, in its essence, is about the need to create and nurture ourselves, so that we have the capacity to nurture and love others. In doing something creative and expressive every day, I'm better able to love those around me. And my family and I are fully deserving of the lighter, more contented version of me. For this reason alone, creativity is so very worth making time for. If creativity is seen as a luxury, we'll inevitably never have time for it. When I make creating a priority, everything in my life flows a little easier. I'm learning that creativity is not a luxury, it's essential for my well-being.

> *"I think of my writing simply in terms of pleasure. It's the most important thing in my life: making things. Much as I love my husband and children, I love them only because I am the person who makes things. I am who I am is the person who has the project of making a thing. And because that person does that all the time, that person is able to love all those other people." - A. S. Byatt*

Chapter Two

LETTING CURIOSITY LEAD

"The guardians of high culture will try to convince you that the arts belong only to a chosen few, but they are wrong and they are also annoying."
- Elizabeth Gilbert

I'm reflecting on a certain irony as I sit down to thrash out this chapter. The first few pages came easily, beginner's luck perhaps? Driven by the novelty of something new, I charged ahead but as I pause now to look around I realise, I'm completely alone. No one's cheering me on from the sidelines. This leads to familiar questions: *What am I doing here? Who am I to be writing a book?!* Imposter syndrome looms large and every doubt I ever had is showing up to stop me in my tracks.

BUT I'M NOT CREATIVE

I was around 11 years old when I first discovered a love for writing. During English lessons at school, I'd get lost down fictional paths of robots and dragon-slayers, wizards and warlocks. I'd relish in the details of the moment but when it came to tying the story together for an ending, I often got lazy. "And then I woke up, only to discover it was all a dream" was my signature move. I just couldn't be bothered to wrap things up properly. I had, and still have, a lot to learn. What I needed was a nurturing voice to guide the way, gentle suggestions to improve. Observations that failure is no bad thing, the lessons themselves too valuable to shy away from. In the words of Clive James, "failure has a function, it asks you if you really want to go on making things".[1] I needed all of this, yet what I got was a public shaming in front of my peers, confirmation of my tendency towards laziness and sniggers from the back of the room. The blush of my cheeks stained so hard that it never fully went away and even now I have to push past those voices in my head, just to be able to show up to my laptop.

My teens were for scrawling poems under the duvet, only to be torn up, lest they saw the light of day. And then I pretty much stopped altogether. I stopped writing for many years. Twenty or more. As I've grappled with grief and trauma in my recent past, the phantom limb from not writing began to weigh heavy. Losing this outlet seemed to add to my feelings of despair. So I decided to try again and began journaling. First with my letters to Charlie and then later with letters to my online community of mailing list subscribers. Not with the intention of selling anything (as is the normal function of a mailing list) but just to flex my writing muscle. I wanted to see if I could put something out into the world that wouldn't make people want to run a mile. To share thoughts. To connect. I've worked steadily at improving, armed with little more than patience and persistence.

Repeated efforts to put ourselves out there definitely requires a few pep-talks in the mirror. The human brain will always take the path of least resistance and pick the easier option. Our brains naturally default to the neural pathways that represent the things we've done before. Creativity emerges when we get off the path of least resistance and give something a go. It takes repeated efforts to form new habits, forge new neural pathways. Writing every day is now my new norm and against all odds, I'm writing a book.

We humans love to think in dichotomies. Just as easy as it is to believe the myth that there's only two types of mum (good ones and bad ones), it's also tempting to believe that we all fall neatly into one of two camps: *creative* or *not creative*. But creation is in our blood. From ancestors who painted cave walls to the toddlers at our feet, the world isn't divided into *creatives* and *non-creatives*. There is only those who use their creativity and those who don't. Picture the messy toddler, frustrated by the colours but determined to paint that rainbow. Good luck prying the brush away as you try to convince him, "this isn't for you, my dear".

Creativity is a habit, not a skill, and it's that daily practice of imperfect trying that brings vitality and positivity to our days.

For those of us who see the value in making but struggle to show up, here's a little gem to carry through your doubting days, one that's grounded in thirteen years of shame research carried out by Brené Brown: "85% of men and women interviewed remembered an event in school that was so shaming that it changed how they thought of themselves for the rest of their lives. For half of the people interviewed, those shame wounds were around creativity."[2]

With such damning evidence, we have to wonder how many others have similar "creativity scars"? How many people are shut down in some way during their formative years, shamed into thinking that they have nothing valuable to contribute? Led to believe they have no place at the table of creation, their only real value being that of the consumer.

Apparently, our natural creative genius is suppressed from the moment we are born. At TEDxTucson, Dr. George Land shocked his audience when he spoke of a creativity test developed for NASA but subsequently used to test school children. The scientists gave the test to 1,600 children between the ages of four and five. Astonishingly, a whopping 98 percent of the children fell in the genius category of imagination. The scientists were so surprised by the result that they decided to test the children again at ten years old. When the subsequent test took place, only 30 percent of the children now fell in the genius category of imagination. When the children were further tested at fifteen years old, the figure had dropped to 12 percent.

So what about the adults? How many of us are still in communication with our creative genius after years spent in the school system? Sadly, only 2 percent. The good news is that the capability we once possessed, never goes away. We just need to tap into it again.[3]

> *"Traditional schooling irons out our creative impulses in order to prepare us for the factory or the cubicle. Our educational system was made this way with the best of intentions, but that way of operating is wildly obsolete."* - Chase Jarvis

Aside from my writing shaming, I remember another moment in my life when, aged around 13 years old, I was belting my adolescent little heart out in the choir. As the joy of singing spilled from my lungs I felt my face rise to meet the air above, as it often did. The music suddenly stopped as my teacher asked me why I felt the need to stick my chin out when I sang. This was promptly followed up with a cruel impression which, of course, made everyone laugh. I sang a little quieter from that moment on, a little more reserved, a little less... me. Doubt took root in my self-confidence rather than my potential.

I've worked hard to embrace my love of singing again. I know now that if I am to sing, I need to do it in a way that brings me joy. And if that means sticking my chin out then I'm OK with that. If people want to laugh when they see me, then I'm fine with that too because to not sing, to deny myself that outlet just isn't an option anymore. Any criticism I receive is a small price to pay for doing what I love and feeling whole. It's the tax on the free lunch because the price is far too high the other way. How refreshing it feels to prioritise wholeness above perfection. Brené Brown writes that creativity is soul-work and boy is she right. It's less about what we do and more about who we are as human beings. She goes on to say that "creativity is the way in which I share my soul with the world and without it, I'm not OK. And without having access to everyone else's, we're not OK."[4]

I shudder to think of something like this happening to my daughter but I know I can't prevent it. Nor should I try to. It's not about shielding her from the world but holding her hand when the inevitable happens. These typical, albeit painful lessons can help us gain greater clarity as to who we are and what really matters in our lives. As long as we are willing to lean into the discomfort instead of running away, we can still earn our place at the table. Leaning wholeheartedly into creativity has helped me nurture resilience and let me tell you, I really need that in my life right now.

So, if creativity is not so much about what we do but who we are, then surely the pressure's off. A soul's expression can't be rated or judged. We just need to get going again. But for those who've wandered so far off the path, how can we rejoin? Maybe you love the idea of doing something creative but don't know where to start or what you might even enjoy. It's been so long after all. Elizabeth Gilbert says we should "create whatever causes a revolution in your heart" but what if you're not exactly sure what that is? When the phrase "do something creative" is just too broad to be helpful, what can we do? Well, let's forget passion, determination and drive for a moment. Take those heavy words which are weighted in expectation off the table and replace them with something far more gentle. Start with curiosity.[5]

FOLLOWING THE CLUES

At the start of 2019 I read *Wabi Sabi* by Beth Kempton.[6] It had been recommended to me by a fellow loss mum in the TFMR community. It was exactly the kind of book I needed to get me through those early days of searing loss.

This book gave me hope. Fast forward 12 months and the landscape of my life and work had completely changed. *Wabi Sabi* didn't exactly light a fire underneath me, it was much gentler than that (and I was too weak and wobbly to handle a fire anyway). It did offer me a lifeline though, a way to move forwards and towards a life I could love when the one I'd pinned my hopes on hadn't worked out.

It's not a book about loss or grief, but about embracing a perfectly imperfect life. Accepting the things that come and go with grace and mindfulness. It's rooted in Japanese culture and wisdom and as I turned the pages, I found myself noting down certain passages that really spoke to me, for what reason I couldn't exactly say. As I read on, I reflected on Beth's writing style, so soothing it felt like a balm for the soul. *What a skill! What a talent!* I thought. Every now and then I sat back and pondered how wonderful it must be to have enough things to say to fill a book. I'd muse on this a little and then get back to my reading and aimless note-taking. Little did I know, I was sewing my own seeds of creation. Plunging my fingers into dark, fertile soil. Allowing myself to be inspired in the gentlest of ways and leaning into it all, in my own small way.

I began to dread the end of the book, worried I'd be

alone with my difficult thoughts again. The moment I finished reading *Wabi Sabi* I decided to put one foot in front of the other. I picked up another book that felt like it might hit a similar spot. More note-taking. I branched out into listening to podcasts, the busy multi-tasking mum's best friend. They slipped into my days with welcome ease. I developed a hunger for the wisdom and inspiration of others. I reached for it. This gathering phase gained momentum and still I had no idea where (if anywhere) it would lead. That wasn't even the point.

"Develop a passion for learning. If you do, you will never cease to grow." - Anthony J. D'Angelo

I was a blank slate in need of source material. I needed proof that survival after traumatic loss was possible. I needed answers to my existential questions. I started reading things I wouldn't normally be drawn to. Non-fiction, thoughts on life and loss, became my topic of choice. I stepped off my usual path, one that might take me away from my present pain. I built a body of evidence that terrible things happen to people and yet somehow, they get through.

Led by intuition, I took each step one at a time, and before I knew it, I was discovering the path to the truest version of myself. I found creative ways to look at the hardest parts of my life, to sit with the discomfort without panic taking hold. Thoughts on creativity and spirituality filled my dark days, flooding them with light.

Over time, input led to output. Writing, music-making, photo-taking, all manner of creative tasks became gradually woven into the fabric of my days. This lit me up from a place within and I never would have made it here, to the point where I'm writing to you now, if I hadn't let my curiosity lead me. We are what we consume, so it's always worth choosing wisely and generously.

The more I think about it, the more I realise that creative self-care has always been there for me when I've needed it, it's just that this time I've needed it so badly that I dared to name it and accept it as an essential part of my life. To quote artist and author Melody Ross, "I finally got desperate enough to create something I really needed".[7]

When I first moved from Brighton to London in 2008, I struggled a fair bit. I was still teaching full-time, working in a challenging secondary school. I was in the death throes of a doomed relationship and as I was new to the city, had no friends to pop round and chivvy me along. One night, I decided on a whim to attend an event called *KaraUke*, which, as I'm sure you've guessed, involves karaoke backed by a ukulele band. It was every bit as silly and raucous as I needed it to be. From that one night, I let my curiosity lead me to beginner ukulele lessons, run by Lorraine Bow, founder of *KaraUke* and her ukulele school *Learn to Uke*.

Groups of us gathered to thrash out simple tunes and cat-howl along. It was a lot of fun. After finishing the course it seemed a shame not to explore more avenues of silly. Before I knew it I was forming a close-harmony, ukulele cabaret act called *The Martini Encounter* along with four other (I'm sure they won't mind me saying) glorious weirdos and misfits. We really had no idea what we were doing. We played and laughed and gradually built a set list which, over the space of five years, rolled out in venues like The Royal Vauxhall Tavern and Latitude Festival. We piled our tiny instruments onto grubby sofas backstage, the stuffing picked out of the seats. We donned wigs and fake lashes in front of greasy, cracked mirrors, scooting around one another in giggles. The cold would bite our ankles but our hearts were hot and happy.

We perched like birds on the edge of the stage, waiting for the compère to raise his arm and waft us out. Out we'd fly, not even really caring what people thought as we opened with our campest versions of "Parklife", "Fat Bottomed Girls", "Holding out for a Hero", and "Sweet Child of Mine". We sang and played and all that mattered in those moments were the creative sparks that flew between us. We stood in the bright lights and made something out of nothing. It was truly glorious. *The*

Martini Encounter was ridiculous and arguably pointless but it brought me so much joy at a time when I needed it. It was also a really good lesson in seeing what's possible when you follow your curiosity by saying *yes* instead of *no* a little more. Curiosity can be as simple as exploring life with an open heart, instead of one governed by fear.

We all have the ability to develop or learn a new skill, at any time in our lives. And as Melinda Gates points out in her book, *The Moment of Lift*, learning is empowering.[8] It can elevate our sense of self and change our future. And what could be more empowering than learning something new that shifts your way of thinking and being into a different direction? Opening up your world to new possibilities feels like a great way to reach for joy.

So if you have a hunch that something that may interest you, go for it! Say *yes* a little more. Take a class, read a book, listen to a podcast on the topic. Pick at the thread of curiosity. The novelty of starting something new will get you going and if it eventually falls by the way, don't be too hard on yourself. Let that guilt go! It's not because you're lazy or unmotivated, you just maybe weren't that into it after all. And that's OK. Allow yourself to explore with an open heart. Flit from flower to flower with grace and ease. Play without purpose. Let the experience itself be reward enough and who knows where it could eventually lead.

"If you're able to step out of what you're comfortable with and what you know, you will be shocked at what it can bring to everything around you." - Kelis

Our children have got it right in so many ways. If we stoop to their world for a moment, get down on our hands and knees and scrabble around after them, we could definitely learn a thing or two. My daughter loves mermaids but she also loves ballerinas and princesses. Sometimes these interests are given space to express themselves individually and sometimes they're mashed together. A cacophony of twinkles and sparkles. Trips around Asda in tutus and fairy wings are fairly standard right now. We do ballet classes, mermaid parties and breakfast in a princess dress. Just like every loving parent, we're supporting each whim and interest.

We fully expect her curiosity to shift and change. As she explores this and that, she's pushing parts of her personality to see what fits. Her fleeting interests fuel her inquisitive nature. And that's a good thing. It's through these interests that Jasmine is developing her creative expression. She wants to dance like a ballerina and sing like Ariel. She's colouring and decorating her bedroom to express herself. Her interests are shaping her in the best possible way. As an added bonus, they even spill over into my own creativity, as I attempt to bake my first mermaid cake in just a few weeks' time.

Austin Kleon talks about the importance of "letting all your weird interests talk to each other". When you have things that interest you, make space for them. Keep them in your life, spend time on them a little each week and eventually they start talking to each other. He goes on to say that "you might not come out of it with a career but what you will come out of it with is a life".⁹ To deny yourself your interests is to lose a part of yourself. Although I'm no longer performing with *The Martini Encounter,* I need to keep the ukulele in my life. It contributes to my feeling whole.

The ukulele also makes an excellent plan B. When I'm stuck with writing, I'll pick it up and strum a few tunes. It's a great way to switch things around whilst still keeping the juices flowing. Doing something with our hands is a great way to kick-start the brain. When I play, I feel a certain grounding, my mind firing up with new connections. Rather than taking anything away, music somehow supports my writing and photography to make it better. Playing also makes my heart happy. If I could summarise this book into a single line, it would probably be: **I think creative hobbies are regenerative and everyone should have several.** There, I said it.

"When we make something, this vast inner resource gets activated, even if the thing we make is simple and small, even if it's a halting, first attempt that is quickly abandoned." - Chase Jarvis

Doing a little bit of this and a little bit of that helps flex the creative muscle. It's also a great way to side-step the dreaded "creative block". There would likely be much less artistic angst in the world if everyone had a tiny, inoffensive instrument to reach for whenever the need arose. A gentle chum to quiet the ego and sit comfortably to hand, ready to jump in at a moment's notice. I'm learning that dabbling in this and that is far better than trying to put all my creative eggs in one basket. Einstein coined the term "combinatory play" whereby he would open up various creative channels to help him work through a difficult equation. He'd pick something where the stakes were lower, like playing the violin, where he could step away from his mathematical puzzles but keep his mind ticking over. After time spent playing, his mind would be clear but sharp, ready to return and solve his problem.[10] In short, he got out of his head by getting into his body.

Starting small is often the best way to jump in. In the immortal words of Maya Angelou, "You can't use up creativity. The more you use, the more you have." Creativity begets creativity. This is where having multiple interests, is really helpful.

When it comes to making, we can't always be all about the output. If we think of our creative efforts as a balloon, we can only ever really breathe out as much as we breathe in. This is where it becomes beneficial to always take in plenty of those deep breaths of fresh-air inspiration.

Apart from learning ukulele, one of my favourite ways to spend those early days in London was to pop along to the Barbican library in my free time. Thumbing oversized books helped me discover photographers I might never have known about and learn from the masters. I could sit for hours in front of the books too big to lug home, pouring over the work of Alex Webb, Diane Arbus, Martin Parr, Robert Frank, William Eccleston, Jacques Henri-Lartigue and Garry Winogrand. I felt so inspired getting to know the work of those who'd gone before and developed a love for street photography that still influences my own images today.

Plenty of input enables the output to flow with greater ease. Creating comes quicker. Thoughts in the shower can be speedily dictated as you drip on the bathroom floor, lines scribbled as you stir the spag bol; iPhone snaps as you side-step the cracks in the pavement, toddler in tow. Making time to make things is no longer even an issue.

"Read a thousand books and your words will flow like a river." - Virginia Woolf

When seeking photography inspiration, it can be really tempting to turn to social media. Instagram is a photographer's playground with peers and industry leaders sharing daily. Trends come thick and fast and when it comes to figuring out my own work I often find the best place to look, is elsewhere.

The social media *feed* is just that. We turn up and tune in to whatever the algorithm wants to show us in that moment. Even the word *feed* implies that we're passive consumers, no control over what we allow ourselves to be fed and therefore, influenced by.

Perhaps it might be better instead, to explore our interests with intention. Typing idea sparks into a search engine to see what comes up, or better yet, visiting a library to devour the wisdom and creativity of those who've gone before. A magpie's eye, scanning dusty archives to spot the gems that others might miss, hoarding original treasures for your very own little pot of inspiration.

As much as I love Instagram, it's for the soul-connections I make there, conversations that have helped me find my tribe. I like to use it to share my work and support the efforts of others, cheering one another as we go. One such person I met there is a lovely lady named Karen. I stumbled across her account through her podcast, *Being Heard*. Each episode Karen chats with women who find themselves returning to work, post-motherhood. *Being Heard* is about hearing your creative calling and searching for career fulfilment, often in a new direction. It's really inspiring stuff.[11] In between listening to Karen's podcast, I'd often see her posting elaborate doodles in her stories. "Day of the Dead" skulls adorned her journal, along with hand-lettered inspirational quotes. As much as I enjoyed seeing her artistry, I must admit I was guilty of sometimes looking at them and thinking *well they're lovely, but she's never going to find her life's purpose if she doesn't stop doodling!*

Then one day, after another scroll-stopping design, it suddenly made sense. I hopped on to message her: "when I look at your drawings, it seems obvious that this is the work that's calling you!". She messaged back to say "funny you should say that because I think I've realised the same! I'm not sure why it never occurred to me before but it feels exciting to think about."

Initially, I'd only seen the hard work that Karen was putting into her podcast. I'd been fooled into thinking that this was where her curiosity was leading her. But clever Karen made sure she always kept this love of hand-lettering in her life and thank goodness she did. She's since opened an online shop selling beautiful and inspiring printables and I'm keen to see where her creativity will lead her next.

It's the doing, not the thinking that holds the value. I honestly don't believe it's possible to work out what we're good at, or even what it is that brings us joy without just going for it. We need to get stuck in and pay attention. Do different things until one or two feel like a good fit. Keep some, lose some, move on. Tweak it and shape it as we go. It's a never-ending process. Taking that first step is everything. It's the only thing that can lead you to the next, and then the next, and then before you know it, you've created a life you love, from scratch.

"For anyone trying to discern what to do with their life: pay attention to what you pay attention to. That's pretty much all the info you need."
- Amy Krause Rosenthal

Chapter Three

THE MINDFUL PHOTOGRAPHER

If writing and music-making are my bits on the side, photography is my husband. Faithful, dependable and there for me no matter what. When my head's all-a-fluff and I don't quite know where to put my thoughts, I pick up my camera and look for the light. Photography grounds me like nothing else. It helps me see what I feel. Drawing out emotions through photos helps me find a proper place for them, rather than keeping them buried in the deepest parts of myself.

"Photography is the story I fail to put into words."
- Destin Sparks

Many photographers will vouch for the deep soul relationship that is possible with a camera. Through shooting often, there's a way to express thoughts and feelings that there's just no way to say. I'm forever taking photos to reflect back at me the things I feel in my soul. Parenting is messy. Parenting after loss, even more so. It's beautiful and painful, gut-busting and heart-bursting. As I try to make sense of life and loss, words often fail me. When words fail me, it's photography that fills the gaps to make me whole again. Taking care of my mental health is at the heart of everything I do these days, for the good of myself as well as my family. Photography just happens to be one of my best tools.

HUMBLE BEGINNINGS

This might seem melodramatic but photography has saved me on more than one occasion. Back in 2008, it saved me from a life I no longer wanted. When I first arrived in London and began working in a challenging secondary school, the thing I'd been trying to ignore for the past four years suddenly became screamingly obvious. I no longer wanted to spend my days working as a teacher. I had wanted to teach young people how to speak Spanish, to nurture a curiosity to travel the world with opportunity and open-hearted exploration. Yet all I seemed to be doing was fire-fighting. Behaviour-management and paperwork. I'm a little in awe of anyone who commits to such circumstances. Where your job comes second to the red tape and unpredictable nature of people. Teachers in challenging schools, healthcare workers; the unsung heroes and the selfless souls, I take my hat off to you.

It was October 2008 that I decided I wanted out. But I also wanted to last the full school year. It just didn't sit right with me to walk away there and then. So that gave me ten months on a full salary to work out what the hell I was going to do instead. Teaching was all I knew. Thoughts of retraining as a translator quickly went out the window as I realised that if I was going to make this huge change, it had to be for something truly worthwhile. I had to create a life I could love.

So long story short, I learned how to be a photographer. I took the hobby that was cheering me up in my spare time and turned it into something I could fill my days with. I let curiosity lead and followed the clues in earnest. By taking a single step, I was able to see the next, and the next, and the next. I found time where there was none. I searched every nook and cranny for stolen moments to build my bridge out of there. Every spare minute was spent working towards my goal to get me out of this unhappy situation as quickly as possible. The 319 bus to Clapham was for consuming podcasts which were a very new and novel thing back then. And Internet learning wasn't what it is today. Evenings were for lurking in forums and asking questions to male tech-heads who seemed to dominate the industry. I began piecing together a wonky puzzle to form a picture that looked like the beginnings of a serious amateur. Weekends, I took myself off to the Barbican library for my academic grounding, shooting all the way there and all the way back for practise. Editing (and learning how to do that too) whenever I could. And when I finally felt confident enough, I took on unpaid second-shooting and studio-assisting jobs. I shined lights on Davina McCall for peanuts as she posed for her aerobics DVD cover shoot. I started to feel that I was getting somewhere.

I saw a chance to step into wedding photography and I took it. In June 2009, I shot my first solo wedding - a friend of a friend - for about £200. My heart was in my throat the whole time. By July 2009, I had the beginnings of a wedding photography business and my freedom. Although it was tough, that year was invaluable to me, it was my runway. One piece of advice I'd give anyone who wants to go for a dream is to think about what your runway might look like. Maybe it's maternity leave funding, reducing your expenses and tightening the belt. Saving every penny until you have a pot that could sustain you for at least three months or get a part-time job. Dreams are absolutely attainable, I just think it's worth being a little smart so we don't end up making things harder for ourselves.

That year on a full teaching salary was my perfect runway, turning adversity into something that could serve me. It meant I could afford to work for the value of gaining experience rather than money. Even after I left that school, I was able to take on a little teaching as a side-income. Supply work days here and there helped me afford the gear I needed to move forward. I didn't ask very much from my budding business back then, only the opportunity to learn and grow. It was a steady growth and no overnight success.

In the same vein, the art of photography itself, learning to see, is no quick thing. The simple and unglamorous truth about photography is that like most things, all you need is practice. No shortcut can compare to patience and persistence, and your camera is just a tool. We wouldn't ask Mary Berry what oven she uses to bake her signature meringues, for we know that the skill lies in her years of experience. Knowing just the right amount of sugar to eggs ratio and exactly how long to whip it for, and in what way. The practice of photography really isn't to learn the camera, it's to learn to see.

LEARNING TO SEE

"The ordinary + extra attention = the extraordinary"
- Austin Kleon

My daughter has a toy camera. It's little more than a piece of wood with a viewfinder and a fake button. She trails behind me in my steps around town and says "click" as she points and shoots at various things. I'm in no hurry to buy her a digital camera because the end result feels less important than the process. She stops to show me colourful gobstoppers packed into her viewfinder, or the cropped legs of a mannequin schoolboy. She gets in close, the tops of his shorts, knees, legs and feet running down her frame. She's noticing all the things that other people hurry past, finding magic in the mundane. Her dad and I often comment that she's one of the most observant people we know. She really sees things. The tiniest ornamental owl on a shelf, on the other side of the room, couldn't escape her eagle eye. She savours life intensely, the visual feast always bringing something to her table. I love that about her so much.

Slowing down to really look at things is where it starts. Asking questions about what we see. *What is the light doing? Where is it coming from? What shapes and colours can I see around me? Is there anything that speaks to me in a way that I just can't put into words?* And if we get into the habit of always taking a camera along, we can step a little closer and take a moment to photograph it.

Paying attention invites playful wonder into our lives in a myriad of ways. It offers us greater opportunity to celebrate our circumstances, as well as the chance to improve our photography skills. Living in East London it would be easy to pop my collar up, wrap my arms around myself and brace against the cold. But if I'm willing to poke my head out and look up, down and all around, there is beauty to be found, everywhere.

The changing light and the direction it's coming from. The deep grey of the concrete on an overcast day. The symmetry of the swings in the park. The flight of the stump-footed pigeons that hang around outside Sainsburys.

Lately I'm making much more of an effort to find magic in the mundane. I'm slowing down to really look. I'm getting in close, embracing the imperfect. Trying to be truly present in the moment. It takes tuning out the noise of the world to really tune in to what's happening in front of us. Meditation, although not everyone's cup of tea, can help us recognise that state of being fully present. Transferring this presence of mind to the way I take photos is as calming as it is effective.

Photography teaches us to see the beauty that many people miss. The shifting light, the curling textures of autumn leaves. The creeping shadows on the pavement so perfectly in sync with the beat of the skipping rope. While everyone else goes about their day, curiosity and wonder has me pulling my car over in unexpected places. Stopping to investigate the patch of backlit dandelions that waive and bob in the breeze, their seeds tantalising close to that moment of escape.

We could always make excuses to leave the camera at home, but what if we tried not to? What if we simply accepted our circumstances and made the best of them? I try to squeeze my camera in alongside the nappy bag whenever I can. If I can't quite manage it that day, I'll shoot with my iPhone instead. The upside of doing this, of making these efforts consistently, is that it pushes me to grow as an artist. When I'm mindful with my camera to slow down and hone in on those pockets of beauty, it makes me that much more appreciative when they appear. Gratitude shooting, if you will. So wherever you're heading, keep your camera or your iPhone to hand. Creativity is rarely convenient, but the time is so very worth wrestling for, even if it has to be snuck in alongside our parenting duties. And it doesn't have to be a huge effort. It can be as simple as making sure you have some sort of camera with you when you leave the house and going to investigate a pocket of light, instead of dismissing it as nothing.

> *"The photographer does the world a great disservice when he leaves his camera at home."*
> *- Mark Denman*

But I get it. The mental load of motherhood demands so much that sometimes even just making it out the door feels like a win. With little ones in tow and the constant requests for snacks, we don't want photography to feel like a burden. This is why slowing down to *really* look is a great idea. Our eyes are open anyway so why not just use them mindfully as we're going about our days. We only have to raise our camera to shoot, when we see something too good to miss. But when shooting, how can we know what will be fruitful exploration and what will be a dead end? Well the honest answer is, we don't always. Having said that, I'm much clearer these days on the sort of images I like to make, which feels like a good place to start from.

At the playground, my friend Ruth asked me, "how do you know what to photograph?". Our chat was cut short because Jasmine was wobbling her way up the climbing frame and needed my assistance. But if we'd had the chance to delve deeper, I think we'd have established that what she was really asking me was, how do I know what *not* to photograph. With a seemingly infinite number of photo opportunities at any given moment, but only a small amount of time at my disposal, I like to get pretty specific on what I'm looking for before I press the shutter. I like to have a process. I'm looking all the time because that costs me nothing, no time at all, but to shoot, I'm a little more selective.

I haven't always worked this way. When I first started taking photography seriously, I found the whole thing overwhelming. So much to shoot, so much practice needed, where on earth to point my eyes first? I used to think that I could photograph anything and everything in all types of light and at all times of the day. These days I have a much firmer grasp on what I enjoy shooting and how best to shoot it. There are certain things that are simply off my radar. Now I'll see them, then dismiss them before continuing the hunt for something I suspect will be more fruitful.

In 2009, I attended a two day workshop with photographer Jeff Ascough. I loved his work because it was so different to every other kind of wedding photography I'd seen. His street photography style was so captivating. The more I looked at his work, the more I realised that I only wanted to shoot weddings if I could shoot them like that. During his workshop, he talked of a process, a way in which he would approach every scene and shoot with intention. He called it the "holy trinity of good photo-making".[1] Over the years, this has become a visual checklist for me, three things that if you take a moment to consider before you press the shutter, can really improve your photos.

Those three things are light, composition and story.

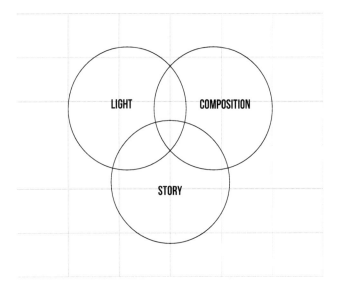

LOOKING FOR LIGHT

For a long time I was content with light and bright in my photos. I'd simply check that the light was good enough (usually flat light) and then put most of my efforts into finding a great composition and story. These days light keeps me lingering much longer. I'd go so far as to say that if the light isn't interesting to me, it might even keep me from taking the photo, no matter how pleasing the other elements might be.

Light is the ultimate metaphor for those of us wading through difficult times. I look for it daily and to my surprise, what I find is that light and bright no longer serves me. The light which interests me these days is usually that which bumps up against the darkness of shadow. I have to wonder why this is. Perhaps it's comforting to be able to see that this kind of darkness is not not only something to be tolerated but also welcomed. That it can actually improve our photos.

Shadow adds soulful beauty, dimension and depth. It brings contrast. Small pockets of light draw our eyes in and heighten emotion. Hazy glows set against a darker background evoke dream-like moods. Slowing down to notice how the light shifts and changes colour through the day is a mindful process, one which grounds us to the moment.

It might sound as though I'm always inspired to shoot but that's definitely not the case. Just like everyone else, sometimes I have to push myself to create. It's true that I find creativity to be restorative and energising, but that doesn't mean I always want to do it. It's kind of like exercise in that way. I know it's good for me but sometimes my brain tries to tell me I shouldn't bother.

Recently, we went away for a bit of winter sun. My headspace was such that one afternoon, all I wanted to do was hide in the hotel room. But I noticed an interesting shadow outside our window. It was around 4pm and the sun was getting lower and lower, ready to wave goodbye to the day. The light was hitting a tree which in turn, projected a dark stretching shadow of branches across the wall. Jasmine was feeding the birds that swooped and fluttered around, their own shadows dancing alongside.

I watched the light shift and move with the setting of the sun. I watched my little girl making friends with the birds. *I'll get it tomorrow*, I thought. *She'll be out there again.* Then somehow I managed to talk myself around. *Just a few frames*, I told myself. *Just 5 minutes.* So I dragged my sorry soul out into the light and did just that. I think we had only 10 minutes before the sun set and the light, this moment, was gone. I felt a little better. I was pleased that I'd done something to change the course of my mood. I felt a little lighter. Grateful for this sweet moment to capture.

When I woke up the next morning and looked out the

window, I realised that this had been my one and only chance to capture that photo. Of course the light was completely changed but also, the hotel staff had filled the space with tables and chairs. They would stay there for the rest of our holiday, making it completely impossible to use the area anymore. I'm glad I made this photo. A gentle reminder to myself that all we really have is now. This is especially true when it comes to light. It's always changing colour and quality.

That photo was taken during golden hour, which is considered by many to be the most favourable time to take photos. It occurs twice a day, the first hour after sunrise and the last hour before the sun sets. With clearer air at the beginning of the day, the light can appear slightly cooler (more blue) in the morning. During evening golden hour, the light can appear a little warmer (more yellow). Shadows are long as the sun skims the earth and spills its yolk across the horizon. Nature really is a marvel.

As much as I love the shadows, I also love backlighting. Backlight is the dreamy, whimsical member of the light family. Taking a photo with your subject in front of the light, so the light is behind them, can create a soft glow. With a little patience and practise, it's possible to create haze or lens flare. Backlight invites us to dance. It's tricky but rewarding. It requires a little physical effort to duck and dive this way and that to explore the angles until there's just enough, and not too much light in the frame. I find it best to capture this type of light during golden hour on sunny days. Obscuring part of the sun somehow though blinds or trees can really help control the amount of light you let in and show the definition of the haze or flare.

I also love overcast light. Pretty lucky really considering I live in the UK. The subtlety of a grey day. The ease of normality. Placing your subject near the edge of a window on an overcast day helps create feathered light which is beautifully soft and delicate. Colours can appear their truest and most beautiful on overcast days. Editing is easier. I love to hunt for colour on a grey day. Complementary pink and yellow, for example, to create drama, or tension within a frame. Or if the mood suits and I'm feeling calm, a more harmonious palette of cool greens and warm blues. It's possible to push and play with those hues in the edit, to tell a story through colour, adding a little extra artistry to the day. Many people overlook the beauty of a grey day- too normal to be nice. But normal feels wonderful to me. When I have days that feel normal and balanced, life feels calm, life is good. So yes, the grey days are alright by me.

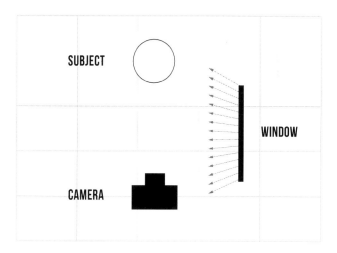

For me, the key to light is recognising the timing. Even when it feels like the light is rubbish, it most likely isn't, it just might not be right for the photos we had in mind. So it's about understanding the light and learning to work with it. Making the most of whatever we have in front of us, can really help our creativity flourish. It's about working with the light you have, rather than the light you wish you had. Our eyes will always have a greater dynamic range than our cameras and when we understand the limitations of our equipment in certain lighting situations, we can start to make creative choices about our exposures. This is when photography starts to become way more interesting.

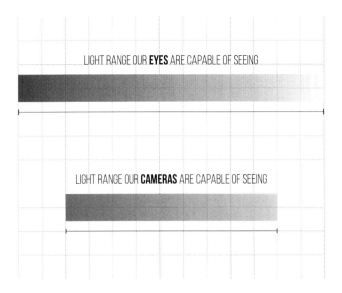

When it comes to creative exposures, did you know that they are possible even with an iPhone? Here's an exercise to get you started. Find a place in your home where there is a patch of light coming through bright and strong. Make sure you choose a scene where there is also some shadow next to the bright highlights. You could look for some light cast by blinds on the floor or find a plant where the sun is hitting only some leaves, leaving others in shade. Now hold your phone up to photograph it. You'll likely notice that the camera will struggle at first, assuming that you want want to reveal the detail of the shadows. The bright parts will look overexposed and the whole thing will look pretty bad. But keeping your camera where it is, tap the screen to lock your focus and exposure. Now drag your fingers downwards. This lowers your exposure. Watch as the shadows get darker, the detail in them falling away. Those bright parts are now properly exposed. Go ahead and snap that photo, then keep practising with other light pockets around your home. Go on a light hunt. Don't worry if you don't have a big camera yet, smartphone cameras can be surprisingly useful in getting to grips with light.

Another practical exercise is to take a few moments to notice what the light is doing at different points of the day in your home. What can you see? Does the light shine through the trees outside to make dappled light patterns on your carpet? Is there a crack of light that sneaks through the bottom blind when you rise for the day? What's happening through the curtains? Can you see the shape of your cat silhouetted there? When does the light in your bedroom appear at its softest and most even? Just jotting down the times of day or year you notice these special moments of light can really help you train your eye to see them before you start to capture them. All it takes is looking.

> *"It's as true today as it ever was: he who seeks beauty will find it." - Bill Cunningham*

COMPOSITION

Composition seems to me to be the nuts and bolts of any photo. It's what holds an image together to help the viewer understand what it is they're seeing. Carefully considering your composition invites the viewer into your world in a way where the path is more obvious. It doesn't always pay to be too cerebral about the arrangement of elements within a frame, but a clear, considered image will always have my heart.

While I think it's important not be too heavily influenced by what others think of your creations, it's great to have a few people whose opinions you really value give you feedback from time to time. Paul is one of those people for me and he never fails to keep me grounded. He isn't afraid to quite bluntly tell me that he doesn't understand what he's seeing when he feels that's the case. Although it stings, sometimes I'll agree with him and this pushes me to further consider the "form" in my photo. It pushes me to work harder, to grow as an artist and further sharpen my skills of expression and connection. The way he challenges me is one of the things I love most about him.

We instinctively know when something looks right. When there's balance or harmony within a frame, we can sense it, although we might not necessarily be able to put our finger on *why*. This is what learning the visual language of composition can bring to our photos. And once we learn the rules, we can choose to break them if we wish. Again, it comes down to intention.

My therapist tells me I have a habit of looking for, as she puts it, "magical signs", and I think she's right. I search for symbolism everywhere. I guess it's my way of seeking order and meaning in the chaos. There are certain visual elements I love to seek out. Horizontal lines for example, ground me to the moment, representing the calm and tranquility I crave. Vertical lines to represent strength, stability and growth. Basically everything I'm striving for. Pops of complementary colours: soulful blue paired with hopeful, optimistic yellow. I'm also always keeping my eyes peeled for interesting shapes and movement, my little girl for example, jumping in a puddle, her buoyant spirit undeterred by the rain.

You might read this and think *what a load of old*

twaddle, but to use my camera and believe that my subconscious seeks these things out brings a strange sort of comfort to me. To be able to express the things I can't quite find the words for feels essential. When you learn this visual language, the world becomes a playground for your treasure hunt, looking for elements to include in your photos.

There are a few firm favourites that I tend to keep my eyes peeled for. Lines: horizontal and vertical, but also leading lines. Negative space, frames within the frame, triangles, rule of thirds. In fact, three of anything is good. Fairy tales and folklore often recognise the power of three: "The Three Little Pigs", "Three Blind Mice", "Goldilocks and the Three Bears". Even Rumpelstiltskin gives the queen three tries to guess his name. Three is the magic number. What are you most drawn to?

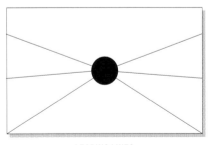

LEADING LINES

NEGATIVE SPACE

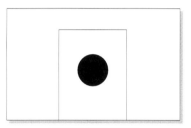

FRAME WITHIN FRAME

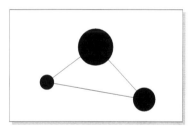

TRIANGLES

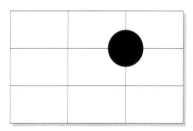

RULE OF THIRDS

STORY

If composition brings "form" to an image, story-telling elements bring "content". I think the sweet spot lies in bringing these two together. It's not always possible and can be really tricky to do this but it does feel great when it happens. "Content" is really just what is happening in the photo. Whether it's two small children holding hands, a boy blowing bubbles or a little girl trying on her unicorn costume, a good photographer pays attention to the details.

Photographer Garry Winogrand famously once said, "Every photograph is a battle of form versus content" and that "great photography is always on the edge of failure."[2] It really is so true, moments happen in the most fleeting of split-seconds and there's always a blink or a weird expression waiting to ruin your image.

Something I do to try to increase my chances of capturing light, form and content all in the same frame is to firstly make sure my camera is set to AI Servo mode (or AF-C for Nikon) and use back button focusing. By holding my finger on that back button, I can track my subject and keep my camera focused on them no matter where they move to. I'll also always shoot in bursts of three frames or more. I can choose the shot that I feel works best when I edit them on my laptop later and it just increases my success rate.

Looking for the narrative in your photos can be as simple as including the wellies by the door on a rainy day, the dripping wet umbrella poised next to them. It might be the spilt flour by the messy mixing bowl or an ice-cream smeared face on a sunny summer's day. Taking a moment to ask ourselves what the story of our life might look like can help us start to seek out these details and eventually, we start to see them everywhere.

When approaching something I want to photograph, I won't look to include anything and everything in the frame, but only the most important elements. I'll consider my subject as key and then mentally step back to work out what else should be included to support the narrative. What else will help me tell my story with this photo? It's not a process of working out what to exclude but being intentional about what I do want to include. Only the most essential things are permitted to stay. I find it helpful to always try to get the crop as close to how I'd like it to be in camera too, rather than losing precious pixels by cropping in post.

Running through this visual checklist in my mind, before I press the shutter, is simply a process. A way to work out the sort of photos I want to take. It helps me work out where to point my camera. First I look for the light, then I look for the composition, then I look for the story. Doing this keeps things simple so that creativity can flourish. It also keeps me from over-shooting and burning myself out.

To be annoyingly contradictory, one of the great things about photography is that actually, there is no right or wrong. Following the signposts to ensure that the light, content and form boxes are ticked can lead to a more engaging image, but sometimes you just have to go with the flow and break the rules. You're creating for yourself after all.

THE GRAFT

Sometimes, the way people talk about photography on social media can make it seem untouchable or unattainable, as they hold their craft in reverence. I used to be so intimidated by the words and photos of others that they would leave me crippled in self-doubt and questioning my worth.

We're exposed to more of other people's finished creations than ever before. We look and admire and then when we create, a lot of the time it might not be that great. Too often we might think that we're just not good enough or talented enough. Yet if you take a moment to look at someone else's cutting room floor, what do you think you'll see? I'll tell you. What you'll find there is a sea of mediocre attempts, the failed experiments and the crappy first drafts. Ira Glass famously talked of "The Gap" that exists in our creative work. If you're not yet familiar with this iconic speech, go and check it out on *Vimeo*. To summarise, his guidance is as follows: When we start something new, all we really have is our taste level. We kind of know what we want to make, but there is a gap that exists between our taste level and our skill level. As a beginner, we make things that perhaps aren't as good as we'd like and feel disappointed. Our great taste, the thing that got us started in the first place, is the same thing that threatens to thwart us. To halt us in our path. Many people give up at this stage. But if you don't give up and keep going, you can begin to bridge the gap between where you are now and where you want to be. The good news is that this is totally normal, we all go through it. The best thing you can do is keep going and make lots of things.[3]

Creativity truly is magic, but that doesn't mean it's not for the masses. It can lift your spirits in unimaginable ways and when you're in the flow, it's easy to believe in some kind of divine intervention. I've seen it happen for myself but I also live the graft. I've taken (and still take) tonnes of photos that suck. But I continue to clock the hours. Over the years I've pressed my shutter button hundreds of thousands of times. And that's the part that really counts. When you're learning, it's the only thing you have any control over. Whether you're willing to show up again and again, tweak your settings, try this angle or that. To slow down and look at the colour and quality of the changing light. To train your eye to spot the visual signposts that point to good photo-making. Tuning in to the story of your life.

Don't kid yourself that creativity only blesses the chosen few. Every photographer you admire puts in the graft. They're learning the language of light, composition, colour and story all the time. They might be more fluent now so the hits come more often but I promise you, we all still have our fair share of misses. So don't overthink it, just crack on with the graft. Don't let anyone's best efforts distract you from whatever it is you need to do to improve. Pick up your camera and take some photos. Try to take it with you when you leave the house. Keep learning, keep shooting. Just keep going and don't let the jaw-dropping creations put you off. You'll get there.

Chapter Four

WHOLEHEARTED CREATIVITY

"Begin with a broken heart" - Pema Chödrön

As mentioned earlier, after my second TFMR, I read *Wabi Sabi* by Beth Kempton. The idea of living a perfectly imperfect life. Her words ignited something in me and if I squinted my eyes, I could see the embers of hope beginning to glow in the dark. When I finished the book, I needed something else. So I let my curiosity lead me to a topic that sparked a little interest, for what reason I really couldn't tell you. Actually, that's not true. With the benefit of hindsight, I do know the reason.

The world of TFMR is shrouded in secrecy and shame. According to the Tommy's website, 2,943 babies were stillborn in 2018 in the UK.[1] The number of TFMR that year was 3269, although this figure is thought to be 2000 short. Each time a termination takes place outside of a hospital, in clinics such as Marie Stopes or BPAS, for example, it is categorised simply, under the broadest term "abortion" rather than TFMR. This means that the total figure is estimated to be around 5269 TFMR each year.[2] That's 14 everyday. Despite this large and shocking figure, the level of awareness is nowhere near the same as other forms of pregnancy loss. The word "abortion" still has great stigma attached and as a result, it's just not talked about. For those who walk this painful path, silence only serves to compound our feelings that maybe it is indeed a shameful thing, a secret to be hidden.

Carrying such a secret makes some women feel suicidal. Some have never told anyone apart from their partners. They pretend to friends and parents that they've had a missed miscarriage. Many women feel so broken from their trauma and grief, that dealing with the shame and judgement on top feels too much to cope with. Instead of facing it head on, they search for ways to bury the hardest truths.

In my lived experience, holding it in is harmful. So we must find ways to let it out. Private or public, it doesn't matter. Write it down, then burn it in the back garden. Watch the black smoke twist and curl as it rises to a place where it can dissipate. Write your baby's name in the sand and let the sea wash it away. Do whatever you can to acknowledge what happened, that you love your baby and that you are deserving of compassion. Write to yourself as you would write to a friend. Be kind. Your baby was poorly and you never asked for any of this.

But it takes time and repeated efforts to work through. Often it also takes counselling or some form of therapy to find lasting peace. And it's no wonder we feel shame. When there are still places in the UK where women must travel under cloak of darkness, often alone and always terrified to end a pregnancy. Their reasons for doing so are so personal and relatable that anyone with an ounce of compassion could understand. At the time of writing this book, termination for non-fatal fetal anomaly remains illegal in Northern Ireland and the Republic of Ireland after 12 weeks. Before first-trimester terminations were legalised in the Republic in January 2019, up to nine Irish women and girls travelled abroad to end their pregnancies every day. While this figure has dropped since then, there are still women being forced to make these journeys.[3] These women go through one of the most traumatic experiences of their life on foreign soil. Afterwards they have to find a way to somehow smuggle their baby's ashes back, because leaving them behind would just be too much to bear.

So given the circumstances, I guess it makes sense that my curiosity would lead me to the work of Brené Brown and her extensive research on the topics of shame and vulnerability.

One very powerful and healing message that resounds through her work is that shame grows in a contained space. She writes, "If you put shame in a Petri dish, it needs three things to grow exponentially: secrecy, silence and judgment. If you put the same amount of shame in a Petri dish and douse it with empathy, it can't survive. Watch to learn what happens when people confront their shame head-on, and why empathy is the most powerful antidote there is."[4]

In short, that thing you keep close to your chest will hurt you. It will spread and wrap its way around your heart to squeeze out every ounce of self-compassion you ever had. To move beyond such difficult and complex emotions, we must first go deeper within ourselves and take a look at what's there.

GO DEEPER WITHIN

Buddhist teacher and author Pema Chödrön offers a very helpful three step process to leaning into the hardest parts of our lives so that we can begin to heal. These steps can be summarised as:

Welcome

Embrace

Accept

Step one asks us to welcome the unwelcome, to acknowledge what we're feeling and turn towards it, instead of turning away. Imagine you are stuck in a Chinese finger trap. With one finger locked in each end, the most natural urge is to try to pull free. You pull and tug and in doing that, the trap tightens and it feels almost impossible to escape. The same principle can be applied to emotional pain. The most natural response is to pull away or to try to block out the difficult feelings somehow. But when we stop struggling and instead turn towards the pain and allow ourselves to be in that space, the trap loosens its grip. Practicing creativity on a daily basis can help us lean in. It offers a safe way to explore very difficult emotions rather than trying to numb them. To refer again to Buddhist teachings, it is possible to see that mindful creativity holds many similarities to meditation.

When I'm taking photos, just like during meditation, difficult thoughts come and go. The trick is not to try to close them off but to acknowledge them, then gently move them away so I can get back to the task in hand. This allows me, over time, to feel increasingly comfortable with the tough stuff. The most powerful lesson I've learned is that negative memories and experiences become less threatening if they are explored in a controlled, calm environment. Traditional meditation can be hard to stick to. Many of us find it challenging to quiet our busy brains enough to commit to regular practice and feel the benefits. I find that creativity offers a comfortable halfway house.

The second step is to embrace; all that we are and all that we wish we could change but can't. Whether it's through painting, writing, dancing, flower-arranging, photography, singing, hand-lettering, whatever it is, allow yourself to be open and honest in your creative work. When we allow ourselves to be vulnerable, to bring the truest, most authentic version of ourselves to our creations, we begin to find self-compassion. How you ask? Pema Chödrön writes that we must "begin with a broken heart", recognising that our vulnerability, our "broken heart" is actually an asset. For vulnerability is linked with the part of us that knows how to love and show compassion.[5] Being open and honest enables us to be seen and emotionally held. So by encouraging ourselves to be vulnerable through our creative work, we're able to find self-love and self-compassion. This is where the healing continues.

Still with me? Good, because this is where things get really interesting. This is where we move towards acceptance. Through a daily practice of making from a place of wholeheartedness, creativity helps me feel closer to my babies who've gone on ahead. I see signs of them everywhere and when I slow down to really look, I find that they never really left. They are in me and all around me. Creativity helps me access that place where they exist again. Creativity turns my losses into a gain, my failings into strength, my hurt into hope. Through creativity I feel like nothing is wasted and nothing is truly lost.

Practicing creativity is a key component of what Brené Brown describes as Wholehearted Living. It brings with it courage and connection. It cultivates compassion, empathy and worthiness.[6] Through these daily efforts, we learn to forgive ourselves. The key word though is practice. Imperfect, repeated practice. For creativity is a habit, not a skill. It's something that needs to be exercised little and often in order for us to feel the benefits over time. It's a path of consciousness and choice. It's about digging deep.

"Only when we are brave enough to explore the darkness will we discover the infinite power of our light." - Brené Brown

But once you turn on the tap, how do you stop the flood of grief? How do you stop it from taking over? The simple answer, you don't.

I think I learned the power of leaning in quite early on. When I found out Charlie wouldn't make it, there was no chance to run and hide. He was still inside me, alive and kicking. Letting me know he existed. I couldn't exactly turn away. When I tried it only seemed to hurt more. There were two weeks between finding out he was poorly to actually delivering him. During those two weeks, time seemed to dissolve completely.

We hid ourselves away, scared to see the bump-touching neighbours who'd smile and ask if we'd found out "what we were having yet". We made our world as small as possible and barely spoke to anyone. It wasn't far off a solitary retreat. Taking that break from the outside world enabled me to look inwards and go deeper within. I felt the full force of it all. The howling grief and the surprising moments of giddy euphoria. The blinding light as I found gratitude that I'd even been blessed with life at all. I felt the full gamut of emotions - a lifetime of parenting pride, worry and love crammed into fourteen days.

It made sense to lean in. Leaning in helped me feel closer to Charlie and make the most of the limited time we had together. Writing in the small hours and meditating with my hands on my belly as the morning light spilled over the slats. Googling photos of stillborn babies at 5am so I wouldn't be too shocked to take photos of my own when he arrived. A crash lesson in hypnobirthing and making playlists to labour to seemed like a good way to go. Leaning in made sense to me.

"I came here to live a life fully, all of it. And I'll take it, I'll take all of it. I just wanna show up for the whole ride." - Elizabeth Gilbert

JOURNALING

It was Sally from ARC who suggested I should write. I owe that group of ladies so much for their support. 4am became my time to write. Unborn babies are usually most active at night and Charlie would always kick me out of bed around that time. I guess the hormones and shock of it all contributed to my lack of sleep and I was grateful for something to do. Doing something with my hands to get out of my head. I began to carry my notebook everywhere, quickly recognising just how much it helped to get things out on paper.

It helped more than anything else. More than talking about it or thinking about it or trying not to think about it. It helped in the small hours when I couldn't sleep and in between the endless hospital appointments. The hours between 4am and 7am were my favourite times to write. In my shrunken world, all was quiet and I found gratitude in simple things like the good weather. I got to see a glorious sunrise almost every morning. My love for autumn light is rooted in Charlie, long shadows and the lingering memory of summer's warmth. That time of year, although painful, will always hold a special place in my heart. It's the season when I feel most inspired, most creative.

"Dear Charlie,

I never really minded the crazy pregnancy insomnia. I got used to lying awake for hours. I'd use that time to plan for our future, learn how best to look after you and find things to buy for you. As the months went on, I looked forward to feeling your little wriggles in the early hours. 4am seems to be your favourite time of day to play with me, I bet you've written "Charlie was here" on the inside of my tummy haven't you? I never minded you keeping me awake with your little kicks and squirms. In fact, I loved them. They made me feel warm and reassured me that, in that moment, you were safe."

I meditated a lot during that time. I'd taken a course and felt a deep connection to Charlie, one that has never really left me. It's reignited every time I write or pick up my camera.

"If we saw grief as holy, so much would change."
- Shelby Forsythia

Organised religion never really did it for me. Where does an agnostic go during times of trouble? When I was desperate for a God I wasn't sure I believed in, I needed to find something else. I felt an insatiable need to mark my experiences somehow, to find meaning and some kind of sacred truth. Following the death of her mother, Cheryl Strayed defines her writing as "the temple I built in my obliterated place".[7] So I guess I'm not the only one who needed somewhere to turn, and in the absence of a formalised, institutionalised, ritualised place, made something up. Something that brought me comfort.

Creativity hits that spot for me and when you're in the flow it's actually very easy to believe in divine intervention. Some days when I'm writing, it feels like I'm just taking dictation from the universe. Or something like that. And I'm not the only person who feels this way. Kooky, I know. I've surprised myself in finding this out.

For me, creativity provides the roadmap to self-discovery. It's the path towards a spiritual and fulfilling life. It also feels like the antidote to consumerist culture. Just as bringing our whole selves improves our creative projects, our creative projects, in turn, serve to make us whole. I find that the more I busy myself with creating, the less I feel the need to "consume". In the simplest of terms, I spend less money in the shops. I also spend less time consuming terrifying news. I don't feel as much need to participate in idle gossip or make judgements of how others are living their lives. By looking inward, I'm able to find the best, most contented version of myself, instead of looking outwards for a validation that never comes.

Creativity is a soul-searchers best friend. Forget whether you're any "good" or not, just go for it. Start today. Start making and permit yourself the intimate exploration of the good, the bad and the downright painful and ultimately, you'll find beauty there.

"People are like stained-glass windows. They sparkle and shine when the sun is out, but when the darkness sets in, their beauty is revealed only if there is a light from within." - Elisabeth Kübler-Ross

For a long time, I thought the idea of journaling had to involve something a little formal. Sitting at a wooden table with an ornate notebook, writing with a fountain pen. Something the cool kids did. I kept telling myself I should try it, try to find the time to sit. Then one day I realised that it didn't need to be anything close to that.

My version of journaling is every bit as messy as my head and heart. I dictate notes and thoughts into my phone whenever they come. I scribble on post-it notes, words and lines here and there. Snatches of song lyrics, Instagram captions. I draft honest letters to my community of subscribers every two weeks, writing down quotes that move me. Lately I've taken to using an app called "Cocoonweaver" as a sort of journaling tool. I can dictate my thoughts and neatly organise them into different topics. My brain needs things to be easy and it's another way to fit creativity into my days. It's been a real revelation for me.

Journaling is a great way to nurture creativity and turn towards those difficult feelings so that we can begin to acknowledge, embrace and accept them. A few lines here and there is all it takes to start flexing that creative muscle and reaping the benefits. If you're keen to try journaling but aren't sure where to start, perhaps try not to overthink it. Just see it as a bit of brain-dump, a chance to notice whatever comes up for you. Single words or full sentences, it all counts.

I guess my journaling started before I even realised that's what it was. Writing has been there all along, it just hasn't happened the way I thought it was supposed to. Fitting something in no matter how scrappy or disjointed is better than not fitting it in at all.

GRATITUDE

"I have always depended on the kindness of strangers." - Blanche DuBois, A Streetcar Named Desire

I grew up on a diet of classic 80s movies. Any devoted *Back to the Future* fans will know that 21st October 2015, was officially *Back to the Future* day. A date plucked from futuristic obscurity by director, Robert Zemeckis. Hitting 88 miles per hour in the DeLorean, Marty McFly would venture forth to rescue his children from a fate that was yet to unfold.[8] I loved those films as a kid and growing up, I'd always wondered what that date would look like for me. What I'd be doing, where I'd be living. It always seemed like such an exciting fantasy. It never occurred to me that this day would hold anything but a wealth of possibility. I'd be 34, the world would surely be my oyster.

By stark contrast, when 21st October 2015 arrived, I found myself walking down hospital corridors, making my way to deliver my son whose life we'd ended via lethal injection two days earlier. I'd started to make funeral arrangements even before he'd been born. Bleached lino floors squeaked beneath me as I walked the white mile to the delivery room. It felt like some kind of sick joke. The near constant stream of women labouring around us seemed endless. One after the other they wailed like banshees and when they finished, their screams fell silent as their babies each began to cry. I continued to put one foot in front of the other, each as heavy as a bag of stones. I listened to those babies cry, knowing full well that my baby wouldn't.

It was then I met Joanne. A wide-eyed midwife with smooth skin on a kind face. An old soul with a true heart. She was young. So young, I worried for her: *you do know this baby isn't going to be born alive, don't you?* I honestly didn't mean it to sound as patronising as that. But she never flinched for a moment. Smiling at us not with pity but kindness. She stayed when we wanted her to and left when we needed her to. She looked after us so well. Joanne was as courageous and wholehearted as they come.

The upside of delivering a baby that won't be born alive is that you're able to access the entire Smörgåsbord of pain relief. Initially I thought I'd brave out the contractions, but before too long I realised I'd been brave enough already. So I began to climb the ladder and into the clouds above.

Morphine accompanied my carefully orchestrated

playlist to labour to. The irony of listening to John Grant's song "GMF" was not lost on me. The music slowed to treacle. It poured into my ears and sweetened my mind with welcome relief. I never felt more at one with my fate than I did in that moment. Warm truths washed over me as I realised I was nothing more than a victim of cruel circumstance. I hadn't done anything to cause this. This wasn't my fault. This was just a very sad situation and I was just doing my best to get through it. Doing my best to make sure my baby never knew suffering. I was taking it all so Charlie didn't have to. John Grant continued to sing: "I am the greatest motherf****r that you're ever gonna meet."[9] The lyrics sank into my sorry core, filling every gap left there by sorrow. Fierce love wears many faces. It's the mothers who lift cars with their bare hands and the ones content on an hour's sleep as they tend to their sick babies. It's those who face each day knowing that a part of their heart is missing, and perhaps the strongest, bravest group of all, the mothers with empty arms. We all have a strength that lurks inside, impossible to know it exists until it's dragged out by its heels.

I drifted until I bumped to the shore. Suddenly it was time. I turned to Paul and said "he's coming" and in almost the same breath he slipped from me and into the world he'd never know. My body lit up with confusion as the standard issue hormones of birth flooded my heart and mind. I felt a bizarre elation and couldn't wait to meet him.

When Joanne handed him to me, she looked me straight in the eye and said "he's beautiful". I could never thank her enough for the way she made my heart swell with a mother's pride in that moment. It was only much later I found out she'd wept when she stepped outside our room. Towards the end of our time together she said what a privilege it had been to be in that moment with us. To lean into the hurt with us. Honestly. That woman is an angel to me. Unfortunately not every encounter with health professionals was positive. Some were, dare I say, even damaging. I've had to find ways to cope with the pain caused by careless words and deficits in empathy.

There's a handful of people I will be forever grateful for. They might be small in number but their capacity for compassion was such that they were all we really needed. Maureen at the fetal medicine unit who spoke slowly and kindly, organising second, third and fourth opinion scans, holding my hand as the needles went in. Dr. Otigbah who took the time to explain what everything meant and waited for me to be OK before continuing. Senior midwife Louise who couldn't believe our treatment up until that point and apologised on everyone's behalf, taking us under her wing from that moment onwards. Our midwife Joanne who delivered Charlie in a way that eased my suffering rather than adding to it. And of course, the ladies at ARC.

Gratitude seems to me a funny thing. When everything

was normal in my life, I didn't really feel the need for gratitude. Why be thankful for something that is just... well...normal? But when the needle swings the other way and we're suddenly plunged into darkness, it rips open our capacity for gratitude, desperate as we become for something good. And if we're fortunate, we become privy to the very best of the human spirit. The ones who want to help us get back to the light and will work tirelessly and often thanklessly to get us there.

Bearing witness to the best of humanity makes me feel very privileged. It's how I'm able to find gratitude in grief and grateful to my babies who've gone on ahead. On my better days it actually feels like an honour to be able to connect with such a profound experience. Hanging on to the belief that there's good in the world, in spite of all the pain and suffering, is how I'm able to wake up and imagine good things happening again. It feels important to feel grateful for this. Gratitude feels essential. So in spite of its shortcomings, I'll always be grateful for the NHS.

And it doesn't end there either. Some of the most important conversations I had following my losses have been with people on the London Underground. Don't get me wrong, I'm not spilling my heart into a tissue every time I commute but little chats happen here and there. London can surprise you like that. When I was pregnant after Charlie, people often couldn't help but ask "is it your first?". Such a casual question that can actually floor many, many women. I got into the habit of searching for a hint of kindness in their faces. Sometimes I'd give the easier, untrue answer of "yes" and we'd trundle through small talk tunnels before I'd smile politely and excuse myself. But If I detected a true heart, I'd be honest and say "no, I had a son but he died". When I took courage in those words, more often than not, I felt lighter and my sharing was met with kindness and empathy. Often these women had their own stories of loss to share, grateful for someone to share them with. Grateful for the chance to say their baby's name again. Some stories were carried for more than 20 years before they arrived at my door. Such conversations are a great reminder that we really never know what someone else is going through, so it's always worth trying to be kind. Through loss I've born witness to the very best of humanity. People who've communicated that very healing message of letting me know I'm not alone. And I'm so grateful for it.

"Humans can be amazing. In the darkest times we get to see the brightest lights." - Matt Haig

Finding gratitude, reaching for it, is so important. Our thoughts both positive and negative, manifest themselves into our reality. The more we allow our pain and suffering to take over, the more it will take over. Believe me when I say I do not want to oversimplify this point. I know that recovering from traumatic loss isn't as simple as putting on a cheery song and being grateful for the chance to dance. But finding gratitude wherever we can, big or small is a way of reaching for hope. I have found that having a daily gratitude practice, finding things to be thankful for every day is essential in bringing the good back into my life.

According to Happify research, writing for a short amount each day in a gratitude journal can increase our happiness.[10] Some people like to start their day this way but I think we can pick whatever times work for us. So I wonder, have you had any moments today when things went a little easier than anticipated? Write them down. Take a second to note the person who held the door as you struggled with your shopping. Maybe you received a kind message from a friend, or even just a moment of calm with a cup of tea. Write these things down, they all count. It's simply a chance to recognise things that have happened, things we've been granted or given, or the things that have improved. And it really is quite powerful.

"Every word we speak and every action we perform affects our future." - Pema Chödrön

Through gratitude and creative living, we have the capacity to change the meaning, change our interpretation of all that's happened. It's possible to work through the hardest times of our life and incorporate them to make something new. Of course I'll always feel sad for what could've been. But I can't change the facts. I can't change the past. What I can have some influence over is the narrative moving forward. What my losses mean to me and how they enrich my life in so many ways. Thanks to my babies who've gone on ahead, I feel more human than I ever felt before.

CONNECTION

I recently watched Peter Jackson's WW1 documentary film *They Shall Not Grow Old*. Veterans spoke openly of their post-war experiences; Coming home to loved ones, grateful to be alive. One veteran spoke of a common feeling amongst those returning, one of a deep loneliness. He categorised everyone in this new and unfamiliar world into two groups - "civilians" and "those who had been in the trenches". There was an unspoken understanding amongst those who'd been in the trenches and palpable relief at being around those who understood. By contrast, spending time with civilians, loved ones, their nearest and dearest, those who hadn't been there, felt hard.[11] There were never enough words to articulate the horrors, no turn of phrase adequate enough to describe what they'd been through. No chance to share the load.

The vast gulf between this man and the "civilians" bears resemblance to my own feelings of disconnection whenever I find myself mentally stuck in the trenches of traumatic loss. Painting a picture is impossible unless you actually paint the picture. Watching this film, it makes all the sense in the world to me that Ehren Tool, mentioned at the start of this book, is so intent on making his pots.

It's not always easy to articulate the things we see and go through in our lives. I often sense that my thoughts and feelings around loss are not welcome in everyday conversation. And fair enough. But through writing and photo-making, I'm able to give a glimpse and lighten the load whenever I need. To slowly build a picture in other people's minds, as well as my own. Cheryl Strayed had something interesting to say around her experience of writing her memoir:[12]

"I wrote about my brother in Wild and he and I had the deepest conversation of our lives after he read it because it gave us a kind of language of intimacy that somehow we hadn't been able to come to in our conversations." - Cheryl Strayed

There's sometimes an ache to share with friends and family, to make them understand. But it can feel like an impossible task. Too big, too sad, too complicated. We want to share but without the looks of pity and horror reflected back. Burying our reality can feel like the easier option. It's tempting to push people away, but this comes with a hefty price tag.

Creativity enables you to find the line between vulnerability and connection. It allows you to share a part of your soul. That thing that feels impossible to put into words, you can shine a light on for the people in your life. Grief is a strange and complicated beast. It goes without saying that what you're going through you wouldn't wish on anyone, but equally, carrying it on your own is very, very lonely. Put simply, creativity offers a way to pass someone the lens for a glimpse at your world. They can look for a moment, then pass it back. It's a way of connecting and starting conversations. It's a way to rejoin the world. Sharing fragments of your soul here and there through creative expression bridges the gap between where you stand and a place of empathy and connection.

FINDING THE LINE

Although I advocate creating from the heart, I don't mean to suggest that we reveal everything. It comes down to a personal choice, but tell-all sharing is something that I generally try to avoid. It feels important to find the line, to figure out what we feel comfortable sharing and set boundaries which align with that. I think it's essential in order to be able to connect with people in a way that is healthy. It's working out what we can share and what we might need to hold back. It's the way I approach things in a way that helps, rather than hinders, my emotional recovery. What we share of ourselves is something we can only learn as we go. Finding the line between honouring our experiences whilst at the same time, protecting our hearts.

For example, I'm comfortable talking about Charlie in these pages because I've processed that part of my life. My other losses are more psychologically and emotionally complicated, with unresolved issues. For that reason, I keep them off the table. Similarly, I might share certain truths online but you'll never see me crying in my Instagram stories. That's just my own line that I don't want to cross. I know what a vulnerability hangover feels like and it usually comes from sharing something, some part of myself that I'm not ready or not OK with sharing. It may even simply be a case of sharing with the wrong person. It's just about finding that line. We can reveal our feelings and still keep certain things off limits if we wish. Remember that this is your healing and you can shape it however you choose.

As a side note, it's perhaps unwise to restrict ourselves during the initial creative process. If we create to heal, it should come freely and openly from the heart. The decision as to what to do with creations, the sharing, comes later.

"Share your stories with the people who've earned the right to hear them." - Brené Brown

In reality there might only be one or two people in your life who've truly earned the right to learn all your stories. You'll know who they are by how you feel after you've shared your truth. When you work out who they are, keep them close to you. Those people are golden.

Sharing online can be subtle and simple. Imagine a 10 second clip of a train slowing into a station, the blistering sun behind it. You might choose a fitting piece of music to accompany and heighten the emotion. Rather than sharing specifics, viewers connect with the mood and atmosphere, as they place their own context and meaning to your tiny creation. And that's OK. We connect over the universal truth, that we all feel things deeply from time to time. Creating spaces to stand together every now and then brings comfort to us all. Sometimes no words are needed. Sometimes in your darkest hours, you just need someone to sit and stare at the wall with you.

When I allow myself to be vulnerable online, it's often met kindly. On one particular day when I shared something, I received a message from a lovely lady named Sophie who has since become a treasured friend, which said: "There are no words but there are better days. And when there aren't better days there will be better moments on those days, however small they are". Those lines were enough to lift me up and carry me through. With a message such as this it's easy to see how being vulnerable brings with it opportunities to heal. How it can truly be the antidote to shame. I'm increasingly grateful for a growing community of like-minded souls, something which has only been possible through striking the balance between sharing and oversharing on social media.

The women I chat to online inspire me daily on my quest for hope and joy in the face of repeated loss. Actually, it's more than that. We inspire and lift one another. Traditional media would love us to believe that women are only out to pull one another's pony tails, as we scrabble and scratch for first place. I don't see much of that in my world. Instead I see wonderful examples of women who lift one another up. I'm eternally grateful for wise words of comfort such as those above. And once again I'm able to see that there are opportunities for gratitude everywhere, even in grief. It's helpful to recognise these moments as our ports in the storm.

So share what you can, when you can, and find your tribe. When you bring your truest self in a way that is open to listening as well as talking, it fosters meaningful connections. Connecting over the topic of loss helps me heal but over time, these conversations have also begun to inform my creative work. Some of the things included in this book, for example, are as a result of conversations I've had with people online. It's a free-flow of feeling and healing, and the very best kind of collaboration.

SOME PRACTICAL TIPS FOR SOCIAL MEDIA

Give more than you expect to receive. Tune out the voices that make you feel like you're not good enough. Widen your interests. Lead with kindness.

"Does this path have a heart? If it does, the path is good; if it doesn't, it is of no use. Both paths lead nowhere; but one has a heart, the other doesn't. One makes for a joyful journey; as long as you follow it, you are one with it. The other will make you curse your life. One makes you strong; the other weakens you." - Carlos Castaneda

Chapter Five

PER ASPERA AD ASTRA

One of my favourite podcasts is *How to Fail with Elizabeth Day*. Each episode, guests are asked to share three incidents in their life where things didn't work out. It's a celebration of all that went wrong and a chance to discuss the merits of failure.[1] If you haven't heard it yet, I highly recommend you check it out.

We're so afraid of failing aren't we? But with a moment to reflect on my own past, I have to say that my most positive life-changing decisions all stemmed from times when things didn't work out.

LESSONS FROM ROCK BOTTOM

My first slap in the face was failing my first year at university. Not just failing and having to do the retakes but failing the retakes and being asked to leave. That was one big fat wake up call I can tell you. Failing that year taught me what it was to really care about my future. It also taught me how to get back up when I failed. I hung around, refusing to pack my bags until I'd gone door to door, asking each of my tutors to reconsider, my desperate knocks yielding nothing in return.

There was one tutor left, right at the end of the corridor, Professor Tim Bergfelder. The only one willing to give a flake like me another chance. I'd be switching from pure Spanish to Spanish and Film Studies. The more I tried to convince him that I'd work harder for this than anything else in my life, the more I convinced myself. I began to change my life, manifesting a new way of being through my thoughts and words. I learned how to learn. I worked a little harder and with a little more focus each day, all too aware of what would happen if I didn't. As I blagged and bluffed my way through the conversation, telling him how much I loved film, that eventually became my reality. In hindsight, this turn of events was the making of my youth and I finished with a 2:1. Sometimes it takes deep discomfort from a situation to find the courage and impetus for change.

From there I sort of fell into education. One day I saw a teacher recruitment advert that seemed to offer a fully-formed career, wrapped in a neatly presented package. The lure of job security and the golden hello. I took the path of least resistance and applied for my

Modern Languages PGCE. Too wet behind the ears to understand the meaning of the phrase "square peg in a round hole" and what it meant to accept a fate that didn't fit.

My first teaching position was in a lovely secondary school in West Sussex. Lovely kids, lovely staff and to my surprise, I was actually quite good at it. I enjoyed finding ways to be creative in my lesson delivery, making up French lyrics to the tune of "Wonderwall" and teaching Spanish numbers through dance. I moved up the ranks to head of my key stage department by the end of my second year. Nothing bad about it at all.

And yet.

I'd often park my car outside the building and shed tears. For what reason exactly, I couldn't tell you. I guess it just didn't really feel like me. There was something inside that I was too afraid to let out. Too scared to let it see the light of day. So unwilling to let anyone else see it that I'd only lift the lid when I was alone in my car. At the start of term, I always felt like I had to put my personality on the shelf. Don the cardboard cutout once again. Put simply, although there were lovely moments, I was living a life I didn't love. Spending precious life minutes on something that didn't bring me enough joy. *Head down and press on*, I told myself. *Work isn't supposed to be enjoyable.* And in moving towards what I thought was right, I moved away from what was right for me.

Looking around it never seemed to affect other teachers the same way. Although they were a bit blue the holidays were over, they really didn't mind being back. They'd found their vocation. Discovered their passion as well as their purpose. Despite the odd existential crisis I could've probably stayed at that school forever. But after three years, I decided to shake things up. To choose courage over comfort and move to London.

"Sometimes I can hear my bones straining under the weight of all the lives I'm not living. - Jonathan Safran Foer

If you're waiting for me to tell you I leapt and the net appeared, I'm afraid I can't do that. Inspiration promises us nothing, only the thrill of the experience. We're guaranteed nothing more than the rush of wind in our faces as we leap off a cliff.

Friends and family thought I was crazy moving to London to work in a challenging secondary school. And maybe I was. The phrase "out of the frying pan and into the fire" springs to mind. During my time there, I got to know some of the most innovative, hardworking and passionate individuals I've ever met. While it should have felt amazing to be in such close proximity to inspiration, it didn't. I felt more out of place and less happy. And the kids were tough. I thought I'd failed. I thought I'd have to turn around and retreat with my tail between my legs. But that move turned out to be an important stepping stone.

I remember one very clear incident where I was breaking up a fight that had started in my classroom. Two girls aged fourteen were determined to destroy one another with hair-pulling and blind hate. In a split-second I dove between them. One of the girls grabbed a chair and raised it above her head with the single intention of crashing it down on her opponent. Caught in the cross-fire, I wrestled with the chair. As it loomed high between us, I had two thoughts. The first was *I hope this doesn't come crashing down on my head* and the second, louder thought was *what the hell am I doing here?!*

The experience was so jarring it forced me to examine my life with microscopic focus. It showed me with absolute clarity what I didn't want. I started there in September and by October I knew I wanted out. I mentally committed myself until the end of the academic year which gave me until the end of July to figure out what the hell I would do next. The gift of this testing time was that it gave me a good hard kick up the bum. From that day onwards, I found a way to hop to the next stepping stone, and the next, and the next, and every one afterwards that led me to where I am now, doing work that I'm excited to get to every day.

As crazy as it sounds, teaching in a tough school taught me how to be a photographer. I did what was asked of me to do my job but beyond that, every evening and spare minute was spent working towards my goal to get me out of that difficult situation as quickly as possible. I'd never felt more driven and alive. I became self-employed and learned the basics of running a business.

I thought I was set for life. I thought I'd see out my days out as a wedding photographer but after Charlie, I never shot another wedding. I just couldn't. Something about them felt too triggering and I realised that I still wanted more from my career too. I began chasing the kind of work that wouldn't be so emotionally charged. High-end/luxury event photography suited me really well. And as I began to pivot, I realised that I was living with greater intention. I only took on client work that excited me. I started to see that whenever I said no to opportunities that didn't serve my goals, I was actually saying yes to something else. I went for the bigger fish, and got them.

Although I struggled with day to day anxiety after losing Charlie, when it came to my work, I suddenly felt kind of fearless. The worst had already happened right? What was there to lose and what could possibly be as scary? I worked on my mindset and built on my existing skills. I learned more about building a brand and developed my event portfolio. And before long I was living the London dream: shooting everything from Vogue dinner parties to Jimmy Choo fashion shows. Kylie, Prince Charles and one of my favourite moments, photographing REM. I was no more experienced or talented than anyone else, I just knew what I wanted.

From there I decided to try my hand at family photography, which felt like the most heart-warming and natural progression when Jasmine was born. Many of the couples whose weddings I'd photographed years earlier now called on me to capture this new chapter of their lives. Lifted by my rainbow, I felt happy and excited to do this.

After my most recent TFMR, everything changed again. I walked away from it all. Nothing seemed to matter anymore. It all just felt so insignificant. For a few weeks, I shut the door on life. Everything was tossed up in the air and only the things that truly mattered to me landed in my lap. And to my surprise, when pieced together, they looked completely unfamiliar. There was no path to guide me, only a feeling. I followed the clues in earnest and now I can honestly say I've never had greater clarity and purpose in my life and work. Empowering and encouraging others to reach for their own creative dreams is my new life mission.

"When you're hurting, one of the best things you can do is go and help someone else who's hurting."
- Joel Osteen

It seems to me that one of the greatest barriers to living a full and joy-filled life is often our self-limiting beliefs. A deep-rooted sense that we're as smart as we will ever be, that our skill set is finite or that what we have right now is all we deserve. But if we so choose, and we believe that it's possible, we can choose to endlessly evolve. Self-limiting beliefs only lead us down a dead-end road. Accepting our lot. Holding ourselves back from pursuing the things we might wish for ourselves. So I have to ask, what would you imagine for yourself if all possibilities were endless? It feels so important, essential even, to be able to do things that light us up, don't you think?

My work is now a perfect fit for my life. It encompasses everything I've learned over the years and I'm able to bring my whole self to it. No more putting my personality on the shelf. All my skills and life experiences, good and bad, feed in to make it the most special thing I've ever done. And I'm not done yet. I know there is still more to learn, more skills to pick up.

Not too long ago, I heard author, speaker and former pastor Rob Bell tell a story of meeting a woman at a gathering in Arizona. She sat down in the empty seat next to him and looked him with absolute swagger and confidence before saying "Rob, my name is Mary, I'm 92 years old and I'm just getting started".[2] How refreshing to see the possibilities even at 92 years old. I don't know about you, but I'm definitely keen to take a leaf out of

Mary's book.

So if there's something you're itching to try, why not just start now in some small way. Root it in who you are. Bring your personality, your skills, your life experiences and explore with an open heart. Be willing to learn more as you go. Take steps to bridge the gap between where you stand now and where you want to be. When what you do starts from who you really are, everything flows a little easier. It's like swimming with the tide rather than against it. And let's face it, when you find the thing that is rooted in you, there really is no one better suited for the job.

Our greatest challenges can often be our greatest teachers. They provide us with valuable chances to reflect, dig a little deeper and ask ourselves big questions like *am I really doing what makes me happy?* Being at rock bottom gives us a chance to change direction, knowing that in all likelihood, the only way is up. It's only through hard times that I've arrived at what feels like the truest version of myself. I feel renewed gratitude for the challenges and devastating losses that have come before, because without them, I might still be sat in a car with a soggy face on my lunch breaks.

"You've got to find a job that makes your heart feel big instead of small" - The Seven Husbands of Evelyn Hugo by Taylor Jenkins Reid

NURTURING RESILIENCE

During those early days after Charlie, Paul and I both noticed a big difference in our behaviour. Our voices became a whisper. We stood close to each other, waiting for the green man to tell us we could cross the road. Too aware of our own mortality. But we only have to look to nature to find proof that there is strength even in our fragility. The delicate shrub is determined to sprout from the wall, no light or life around it. It wavers in the wind having forced and pushed its way through concrete. Creation is a marvel and we are all much more capable of resilience than we give ourselves credit for.

Grounding techniques were helpful day to day but I hated feeling meek. As grateful as I was for compassion, I hated the pity. None of us really need pity. We need strength. And for me, finding strength and resilience comes from creative living, from flexing and working that muscle a little bit every day.

Choosing a life of making things, especially if you decide to regularly show up and share them, requires a certain amount of toughening up. Because here's the truth, being creative doesn't hold any promise that what we make will be any good. We're conditioned to confuse *being creative* with being *artistically good* at something, but in my mind that's not it at all.

My friend Ruth messaged me recently to tell me she

was baking a cake. She said something along the lines of "Look, I know you talk a lot about creativity and the mental satisfaction that can come from making something, but I'm baking my daughter's birthday cake and it's bad. I mean, really, really bad. So perhaps the other side to your argument is that occasionally you look at what you've made and realise you're not very good and so maybe...outsource?"

I needed some evidence of this terrible cake. A photo followed shortly after and I have to say that it wasn't that bad. It had wonky charm aplenty and I bet it tasted great. But that's not even the point. We can get better at anything if we stick with it enough, but being a bit crap in our creative work holds value in itself, even in the unlikely event we fail to improve.

We make things based on our taste levels and the things we aspire to make but a lot of the time, they might not be that good. But even though the end result might not turn out as we hope, that doesn't change the fact that the simple act of making something, will have affected us positively in some way. If you tend to your creative outlets regularly, make things, big or small, regardless of the outcome, the better you'll be for it. Creativity offers a way to practise coping with the small things, to better cope with the big things. It's life in a microcosm. Carrying on regardless promotes resilience. As human beings as well as creatives.

Remembering that creativity is a habit and not a skill gives us permission to stick with it when the going gets tough. To keep trying even though every now and then we make something less than perfect. Holding on to the habit, valuing the process over the end product feels like the right approach.

Creativity offers a safe space to practise being OK with imperfection. And I think we could all use a little of that. At a time when it can be easy to look online and believe that everyone else is living a perfect life, I believe that the antidote is to get on with making something, regardless of the outcome. Rather than sitting around and indulging in negative thoughts, go make some bad art, then make some more. Let's learn to sit in the discomfort of our own imperfection. Enjoy the successes when they come but learn to push on through when they don't. It really is good for us.

By regularly embracing imperfection through our creative efforts, big or small, we start to send signals to our brains that say: so *what if you're no good this? It really doesn't matter.* Carrying on regardless has the power to change our way of thinking. New neural pathways are formed. Falling down and getting back up again and again convinces your brain that you are strong and resilient. It doesn't matter that all you were doing at the time was crocheting a doily. Your brain doesn't care about the context, only the fact that you took courage and carried on when it went horribly wrong.

Let's look again to our children for inspiration. Watch them in their own creative work, the drawing and the tower-building. They aren't beaten down by the failed attempts, it's just part of the learning and brain growing. No one tells them to try again, they just do it naturally. It's instinctive. They unconsciously know it's good for them to do this.

Repeated acts of creative courage are good for us all. Over time this courage eventually spills from your creative work and into your life, with nowhere else for it to go. You begin to feel braver and less broken. Choosing a path where occasional failure is inevitable is so very helpful in nurturing resilience.

It doesn't have to be huge acts of courage, like bungee-jumping off a bridge. Just tiny, daily acts to make us feel a little bit braver, a little bit stronger. A little bit more capable of surviving and getting back up no matter what life throws our way.

Creativity is both my mental sanctuary and my courage. It helps me organise my thoughts, accept my truth and teaches me to be brave. Although I know I will definitely make mistakes along the way, the only real failure will be if I give up. It feels like a great way to strive for a life well-lived.

SURVIVING, THEN THRIVING

"First it hurts, then it changes you." - Unknown

I'm fascinated by the story of *Frozen*. Elsa, our protagonist, holds a dark and icy secret. She tries to quash and conceal it. All this does is make things worse. She feels grief, anger, bitterness and despair. Pain is rooted in the resistance of her truth.[3]

When Elsa embraces her reality and accepts the hardest parts of her life, she's suddenly able to harness her power and do amazing things. Things that most could only dream of. This story always gets me thinking about the overwhelming emotional energies created through profound loss. Anger, longing, despair....Where does all that unspent energy go? What if we could harness its great power? What if we could somehow tame the wild horse that rides inside? What if we could become the grief-whisperers of our souls? What if we could channel that rare, unique energy into something that could serve us or the good of our communities?

The thing is, we already see this often. So many loss parents do this. They cross oceans in the name of their children, climb mountains, fundraise, change laws. The unstoppable force of love fuelling their every step. When you couple the energy of loss with the lightning bolt realisation that life is precious and short, you slowly come to realise that we're all capable of pretty much anything we dare to dream. So as weird as it sounds, I'm more and more convinced that grief might just be the source of my superpower.

"What the caterpillar calls the end of the world, the master calls a butterfly." - *Richard Bach*

I learned something pretty amazing recently. I always thought that when a caterpillar retreats to the cocoon, it simply grows wings. But this is only a small part of it. To begin with, the caterpillar almost entirely dissolves itself. It melts and breaks down all but the most essential parts, in order to make way for new building blocks of life and form. Only then can the caterpillar begin to transform, grow wings and become the butterfly. Destruction of the old is an entirely necessary step on the path to transformation.

After my second TFMR at the end of 2018, I cocooned myself away. Melted down by grief and anxiety, I was undone. I needed things to be as simple as possible for a while. I needed time and I needed space. Acceptance, meaning and thriving were so very far off my radar at that point. And who could blame me? I've since learned that this is quite normal for situations where everything has been impacted by change. Author and speaker

Martha Beck refers to this time as "stage one", the stage of death and rebirth, where everything falls apart. When the world you know is destroyed, a new world must be created.[4]

When the days eventually stopped blurring into one, I began to construct a tiny, light-filled world around myself. Nourished and transformed by my own cocoon, I read, listened to inspiring podcasts, wrote and took photos. I learned a few things online and then I learned some more. I hoarded quotes that carried the kind of language I wanted and needed in my life. I took the broken pieces and rebuilt myself in a different way.

I'm writing this final chapter in late March of 2020, a time that will go down in history as the advent of the COVID-19 pandemic. Over the past few weeks, we all felt some kind of grief as we came to terms with the loss of the world we once knew. And no one yet knows how it will end. The only certainty right now is that for the foreseeable future, we're all being asked to cocoon ourselves away.

The cocoon is, by definition, a safe container, a place to withdraw to. It might be a home or it might simply be a routine. A series of daily actions to cling to, offering the structure and stability required when reality knocks hard.

When lockdown rolled out across the globe, it was

interesting to note how quickly the message of "use this time to better yourself" sounded out across the Internet. Endless offers to learn a new skill seemed like a quick fix. "5 Steps to Cope with Loss" posts advocate a simple process, a formula. But I find this message too clinical to be helpful, and missing something vital. Something that can't be bought nor sold: the time, space and permission to feel things.

It seems wrong to gloss over the complexities of the human condition. As many of us lurched into emotional chaos at the start of the pandemic, I felt myself returning to ground zero once again. You see, even with the most secure practices, resilience isn't always immediately possible. It often takes time, perspective and a safe distance to build (or rebuild) that muscle. It takes looking after yourself and allowing yourself to feel. When first faced with shock and uncertainty, we're lucky if we get a full night's sleep. In such circumstances, who wouldn't need to spend some time adjusting?

Bouncing into thriving, by-passing the hurt just isn't a realistic expectation. We need time to feel and reel from loss. For some of us at the end of March 2020 it was the loss of our freedom, proximity to relatives, physical connection. For others it was financial stability or the very real, actual loss of loved ones. For young people it might have been the loss of the last summer with their school friends. We all grieved the loss of the world we once knew. The loss of our "normal". And to get tangled up in the "my grief is worse than your grief" game is a race to the bottom. For whenever we dare to play, winning just means losing.

Here are a few things I've learned about grief. Firstly, all grief is valid. All feelings are valid. Your loss will always be the worst because it's yours.[5] You're entitled to it, so allow yourself to feel it. Grief is messy and nonlinear. It's rare for any two people to experience it the same way. There's no right or wrong and there's also no end. This isn't necessarily a bad or scary thing. As Nora McInerny says in her incredible TED talk, "we don't move on from grief, we move forward with it".[6] I've found this to be an incredible way to reframe the hurt.

When plunged into darkest waters, we feel the full force. If we fight and kick straight away, disorientated, we'll likely head for the ocean floor. Allowing time feels sensible, at least to begin with. To let calm limbs and compliance work with the water, rather than against it. To give our bodies a chance to float up so we can again catch our breath.

But when at last we find ourselves bobbing on the surface and we feel the urge to swim for land, the strength required to get there can be enough to change our lives forever. The clarity of thought, effort and focus needed can be such that when you eventually arrive at the shore, you may well find you have a new way of working with your mind and an entirely new outlook on life.

I'm reminded again and again that there is no foolproof way to cope with whatever life throws at us, but it sure helps to have an awareness. Staying mindful, present and connected to the moment, and how we're feeling, gives us the best chance to float to the top, then swim for new shores.

When returning to your old life isn't an option, it's my belief that creativity holds the key to moving forward. Creating a life you can love. Acceptance is largely acknowledged to be the most coveted stage of grief but for me, acceptance is never enough. For me, there has to be meaning. Creating a life I love in spite of the hurt helps me find meaning from loss.

If you've ever gone through something awful, chances are someone at some point will have said to you "everything happens for a reason". As a bereaved parent I can't tell you how much these words upset me. It's my belief that things don't happen for a reason. Sometimes terrible things happen for no reason at all but such incidents can be powerful enough to help us find meaning beyond the terrible event and because of it. I think it's this that confuses people into thinking that the death of your loved one held some mythical, magical power, but in my mind it's not that at all. The meaning lies within us. It's what we do afterwards that counts.

When I was around 14 years old, every now and then my PE teacher would inflict cross-country running on us. I absolutely hated it. It was difficult, sweaty and uncomfortable. The course would take us on country lanes through peaks and troughs and seemingly went on for miles. I always skulked to the back of the group with the other quitters and took my sweet time. I was quite content in my comfort zone thank you very much. As a result I never got fitter. I never understood the value of exercise and what it could bring to my life.

Had I pushed myself a little more, breathed through the burn, raised my shoulders and pushed up the hills, over time, I would've become stronger and more focused. The fuzzy patterns in my eyes would've faded away, the spots replaced by crystal clarity and best of all, endorphins. What I didn't understand then, was that fitness wasn't simply a gift bestowed on a chosen few, it was something that took concerted and consistent efforts to build up. To get to a place of increased fitness, you have to make life difficult for your body for a while. When you're no longer in that zone of comfort there's a call for more strength.

Eckhart Tolle states that "when life becomes difficult for a human being, there's a demand for a greater consciousness to overcome the difficulties".[7] So in essence, although it's hard to believe, adversity, in all its forms, often holds great value. There's a Latin phrase which goes back 2000 years: "per aspera ad astra" which means "through hardships to the stars". This age-old wisdom helps us creatively reframe life's obstacles and challenges. It encourages us to push beyond what we think we can manage, and grow.

Grief, trauma, the hardest parts of our lives can often present such opportunities for growth. When I look back, I can say with absolute certainty that my biggest leaps in life all stemmed from deeply challenging times. Tolle continues, "things do not evolve from comfort zones. The obstacle has an essential function, it forces us to generate more strength/energy/consciousness." Soul-searching and a burning need to find greater meaning helps us overcome these obstacles, and all we have to do is keep following the clues with curiosity and an open heart. Strength over time leads to power and optimism as we dig deep and ultimately emerge stronger than ever.

We have to accept things before we can change them. Many people spend their whole lives simply wishing for something else but never taking any real action. Acceptance is all too often mistaken for the final stage but in my mind it's really just another first step. Beyond acceptance, what would you reach for? I want my life to be filled with creative possibilities. I want to teach my daughter to be curious, compassionate and courageous. I want each day to feel hopeful. We're presented with the myth that there's only one way of living. The safe way. The 9-5. But as we're all beginning to experience first-hand, safety is merely an illusion. The path has never been more obscured. Although we have no maps, we still have our inner-compass, feeling out the next step, one at a time.

When things are "normal", it's tempting to avoid the unknown. We're afraid of it because it lies outside of our comfort or control. But when we're thrown off our path in times of trouble, we're plunged into the abyss regardless. And when the worst happens, what else is there to lose? The things that break us can also be the things that make us.

> *"Terrible things can happen to us. We can not only endure them but survive them and allow them to shape us into something very interesting in the alchemy of our growth." - Elizabeth Gilbert*

Per Aspera Ad Astra

CONCLUSION

"Help me make the most of freedom and of pleasure, nothing ever lasts forever." - Tears for Fears

Have you ever seen the *HBO* Series *Six Feet Under*? I've recently been bingeing my box set for the umpteenth time. If you feel like you're in need of some grief therapy but just can't afford it, may I suggest you watch this show. It's completely unashamed to show the dark, painful side of life, without being depressing or nihilistic. It's provocative, macabre, witty and sincere. I love it.

There are so many profound moments but one that really stood out to me was when one of the characters, Tracy, asks "why do people have to die?" and Nate, taking a moment, replies "To make life important. None of us know how long we've got which is why we have to make each day matter. A life well-lived. That's the most any of us can hope for."[1]

I'm the kind of person who likes to rewind moments like these in TV shows and films just to hear the words again and again until they permeate my understanding of the world. I can be a bit of a nightmare to watch things with.

Embracing impermanence has become a driving force in my life and work. The knowledge that nothing lasts forever might seem sad but I really think the power is in the perspective. To turn things on their head, I find comfort in knowing that even on my darkest days, the sun will shine again. Through creativity, it's possible to change the meaning of impermanence from something sad to something hope-filled and meaningful. To help us treasure the time we have and live with greater intention. To make choices that matter. To be a little braver. Without profound loss I'm not sure I would have had such realisations and opportunities to grow.

We can half-live our lives, holding back in fear or we can accept the ever-changing nature of all things and lean in. We can allow life's stark contrasts to wash over us and shape us over time like chequered rocks on a vast beach. The light and the dark, the joy and the sorrow, the bitter and the sweet.

So how might a well-lived life look and feel for you? I'll tell you my version of hope, in case it's helpful. Mine is filling my days with creative possibility and purpose, pushing beyond the self-limiting doubts and reaching for things that matter and mean something to me. It's using my voice. It's being my own boss. Striving to be ten times more magnanimous than I believe myself capable of being. Having the courage to write a book and share my truth. Helping others reach for their own creative dreams. It's being a loving mum and partner, whilst still making time for me.

It's not always possible to know the "how" straight away, but as long we're willing to explore and find ways to jump the hurdles when they arise, we can keep going. Some hurdles will be bigger than others. The creative journey is always going to be a work in progress because those self-limiting doubts are deep rooted in us all, myself included.

Whatever our stories, it's my belief that through creative living, it's possible to find a renewed and hopeful sense of strength, along with a new perspective. A new appreciation for life. These days I have a strange feeling that my own life is fuller and richer because of my losses. I'm hesitant to use the word "better" because who would choose a life of profound loss? Of course I would rather have my children by my side. I can't change what's happened, but I can affect what happens next. And I'm grateful for this insight. For the removal of apathy and settling. For the chance to dig deep and discover what I'm made of.

There is something about being able to create, even

when I feel as though I'm failing at creating life, that's very empowering. When my maternal instincts can't be fulfilled by things out of my control, it's my daily practice of making that helps me through. Order is restored each day, day after day. When I do this, I feel no longer broken and I am once again the source of creativity.

And the world needs your creativity too. We need your gifts and your unique contribution. There are too many of us overwhelmed and underwhelmed by life and I don't believe it needs to stay this way. What if you are holding something back that might just be the key to unlocking someone else's healing? What if you have a very particular way of articulating or capturing something that could help someone else? What if you hold the mirror that helps another person really see themselves? What if your story proves to be someone else's survival guide?

"When we women can use our talent and energy, we begin to speak in our own voices for our own values, and that makes everybody's life better."
- Melinda Gates

With efforts to move beyond the initial fires of suffering:
- empowering yourself through learning, making time where there once was none, failed attempts that build

your resilience and teach you valuable lessons, the ability to show yourself compassion and carry on regardless; this is what it means to me to live creatively. But it's a marathon not a sprint. These muscles need time to strengthen, new habits need time to form. But a little every day and the gentle commitment to a new practice, a new way of life, in years to come you'll be so glad you started now.

"The best time to plant a tree was 20 years ago. The second best time is now." - Chinese proverb

So take that first step then take another. If the path doesn't really interest you, try a different one. Stay curious and dig deep. Act bravely on the knowledge of who you truly are. Feel your losses fully and use that energy not to escape your reality but to embrace it and make something new for yourself. To live the truest, most beautiful life you can imagine. Feel it and use it. This rallying cry is to encourage you to honour your pain and your hurt. Your life, your love, your loss. All that you are. You can honour everything through creativity and find your way home.

Workbook

THE PRACTICAL "HOW TO" BIT

If my background in teaching has taught me anything, it's that nothing ever changes through thought alone. It takes action to move forward.

The following pages are intended to offer a little hands-on guidance to help you put into practice some of the steps outlined in this book.

I hope you find them useful. More resources can be found at www.mylittlemuse.co.uk/rallyingcryresources

Chapter One

CREATIVE SELF-CARE

WHAT?

Which creative outlets spark interest for you? List 2-3 interests or hobbies you would like to explore further.

1.

_____

2.

_____

3.

_____

HOW?

Write down your non-negotiables in terms of time. What do you have to/want to do, no matter what?

Then write down anything in your week where you could shave a little time off for your creativity. Remember, we don't find time, we *make* time.

Non-negotiables

_____

_____

_____

_____

Time Opportunities

_____

_____

_____

_____

If you're struggling with this and would like a little more guidance, I created a free creative self-care planner, which you can download from:

www.mylittlemuse.co.uk/rallyingcryresources

BARRIERS

Do you put off certain creative tasks or activities? Try journaling some thoughts around why this might be. If you can't immediately think of anything, dig a little deeper into your memories. Was your creative curiosity nurtured as a child? How were the conversations around creativity in your home and school life? Taking this step is really important so we can actively acknowledge and begin to live beyond any self-limiting beliefs.

Chapter Two

LETTING CURIOSITY LEAD

Nourish your mind. List 2-3 books, podcasts or courses you might like to try. Pay attention to how the content makes you *feel*. For any books you enjoy, search the "books you may like" section on Amazon. Add them to your read list.

Books

_____

_____

_____

_____

_____

Podcasts

_____

_____

_____

_____

_____

Courses

_____

_____

_____

_____

_____

INSPIRING QUOTES

Write down any quotes that move or inspire you, as you naturally find them. Quote searching online will usually just result in words you've heard and read a thousand times before. They won't hold any real meaning for you. The best ones are hidden in the content you already love.

When you stumble across a great quote by chance, research who said it and see what more you can find out about this person and what else they have created in the world. Consume more of their work.

WORDS THAT SPARK CURIOSITY

Come across an interesting word? Has is sparked your curiosity? Hoard it for later. Don't think about how you might use it, just stash it for now. Not sure what it means? Google the definition, explore synonyms.

Word _____

Meaning _____

Synonym _____

Word _____

Meaning _____

Synonym _____

Word _____

Meaning _____

Synonym _____

List 3 more ways you could feed your imagination over the next few months.

1. _____

_____

_____

_____

2. _____

_____

_____

_____

3. _____

_____

_____

_____

Chapter Three

THE MINDFUL PHOTOGRAPHER

Photos to accompany this chapter can be found at www.mylittlemuse.co.uk/rallyingcryresources

LIGHT

BEGINNER ACTIVITY: *MAKE A CREATIVE EXPOSURE WITH YOUR IPHONE*

1) Find a place in your home where there is a **patch of light** coming through bright and strong. Make sure you choose a scene where there is also some shadow next to the bright highlights. You could look for some light cast by blinds on the floor or find a plant where the sun is hitting only some leaves, leaving others in shade.

2) Now **hold your phone up to photograph it**. You'll likely notice that the camera will struggle at first, assuming that you want want to reveal the detail of the shadows. The bright parts will look overexposed and the whole thing will look pretty bad.

3) Keeping your camera where it is, **tap the screen to lock your focus and exposure.**

4) Now **drag your fingers downwards**. This lowers your exposure. Watch as the shadows get darker, the detail in them falling away. Those bright parts are now properly exposed.

5) Go ahead and **snap that photo**, then keep practising with other light pockets around your home. **Go on a light hunt**.

INTERMEDIATE ACTIVITY: THE BACKLIGHT DANCE

1) During golden hour, shoot with the **sun behind your subject** and look for something that can **block some of the light**. e.g. a tree, a house, a mountain or your subject themselves.

2) Using your DSLR in manual mode, **meter** for the elements in your frame that you would like to expose for and then make **very small corrections** with your body so that that the sun is peaking through at varying degrees. Find the sweet spot by dancing the backlight dance, shooting a few frames here and there as you go. **Bend your knees, bob this way and that** until there is just enough, and not too much light in your frame. Play. Experiment. Dance.

BONUS TIP:

For flare - use a wider lens, preferably a zoom (as there is more glass for the light to refract through) and a higher f-stop.

For haze - Use a longer focal length and lower f-stop. Primes lenses are great for haze.

COMPOSITION

BEGINNER ACTIVITY: RESEARCH SOME COMPOSITIONAL ELEMENTS FROM THE FOLLOWING LIST:

Leading lines
Horizontal lines
Vertical lines
Negative space
Odd numbers
Rule of thirds
Framing
Golden ratio
Perspective/viewpoint
Symmetry
Patterns
Creating depth with foreground, middle ground and background

Google them or search for them on Pinterest. Note down 2-3 that you will try to incorporate over the next few weeks.

1.

_____

2.

_____

3.

_____

INTERMEDIATE ACTIVITY: TRIANGLES EVERYWHERE

Incorporating triangles is a great way to fill your frame, create balance and add movement in your images. Look at some of your favourite photos and notice how your eye moves around the frame. Pay attention to where your eye naturally lands first, then notice where it goes next.

Good composition tends to lead our eyes around the frame in a triangular motion. Stronger composition incorporates multiple triangles - when you feel your gaze moving hungrily around a frame, it's likely moving in triangles. Knowing this is powerful stuff. With this in mind, how might you try to nurture more visual movement in your images through triangles?

Visit www.mylittlemuse.co.uk/rallyingcryresources to see some examples of this in action.

STORY

BEGINNER ACTIVITY: DETAILS

Think about your everyday activities and the "details" that support them. For example: brushing teeth, tying shoelaces, breakfast time, trips to the playground. List these activities below. Could you include any storytelling details to support the narrative of your photos?

EVERYDAY ACTIVITY	STORYTELLING DETAIL
e.g. brushing teeth	toothbrush, sink, toothpaste, messy mouth etc.

INTERMEDIATE ACTIVITY: BACK BUTTON FOCUS

When your DSLR comes out of the box, the default settings make it so your shutter button has two functions:

1. Focussing (half-pressing)
2. Taking the photo (full-pressing)

One button having to do two jobs is not ideal. Back button focussing is when you seperate the two functions out so that they each have a button of their own.

When you do this, you allocate the job of focus to a button on the back of the camera. Now your shutter button's only job is to take the photo. I find shooting this way helps me stay reactive to those split-second moments and better control focus.

If your camera is capable of back button focus, it's just a case of going into your settings menu and switching things around.

Check out your camera model to see if you're able to change the settings to back button focus if you haven't already. A quick google along the lines of "how to set back button focus for <insert camera model>" should help with this. You'll only need to set it up once and if you're not keen you can always change it back.

Back button focus can help capture those fleeting, never-to-be-repeated moments. To strengthen your chances, use AI Servo (Canon) / AF-C (Nikon) and shoot in bursts of three frames or more.

Chapter Four

WHOLEHEARTED CREATIVITY

List 3 ways you could bring more mindfulness to your mornings.

1. _____

_____

2. _____

_____

3. _____

_____

If you'd like to try some Buddhist meditation, I've included some simple steps here that are steeped in compassion and healing:

THE FIVE STAGES OF METTA BHAVANA

Metta Bhavana is about cultivating an emotion, something you feel in your heart. "Metta" means love (non-romantic), friendliness, or kindness and "bhavana" means development. There are five stages of this practice and it's best to aim for around 5 minutes for each stage.

1. Yourself - In the first stage, you feel "metta" for yourself. Try to become aware of your mind, and focus on feelings of peace, calm, and tranquility. Let these grow into feelings of strength and confidence, that then develop into love within your heart. Close your eyes and breathe deeply while repeating these words in your mind:

"May I be well,

may I be happy,

may I be free from suffering,

may I progress."

This repetition is a way of encouraging the feelings of "metta" for yourself.

2. A friend - Just as you encouraged feelings of "metta" for yourself, now do this for a friend. Picture them in your mind with those same positive thoughts and feelings and repeat the words with the subtle change:

"May he/she be well,

may he/she be happy,

may he/she be free from suffering,

may he/she progress"

3. An acquaintance - Repeat the practice for an acquaintance. Someone you have neutral feelings for. Include them in your feelings of "metta", using the words to anchor your mind.

4. Someone you dislike - This one can be tough because you need to think of someone you're having trouble getting along with and include them in your feelings of "metta". It's important to extend kindness to them even though it may feel difficult or uncomfortable. Repeat those same words with positivity for that person.

5. Everyone - Now using the words *"may they be well, may they be happy…"* think of all four people together and the wider world. Extend your feelings of loving kindness to all and then gradually relax out of meditation, bringing your practice to an end.

GRATITUDE JOURNALING

I like to keep my journaling prompts simple, with just a few. If you'd like to try this, simply pick a time that works for you and write down each day:

1. Something that went a little easier than anticipated

2. Something that made you smile

3. The best thing about the day

4. Something you're feeling more hopeful about

Gratitude journaling is simply a chance to recognise things that have happened, things we've been granted or given, or things that have improved. Try to be specific. It's great to do this daily. Even if you don't quite make it to writing these things down, try to take at least a moment in your day to reflect on them. It really is quite powerful.

Chapter Five

PER ASPERA AD ASTRA

Time now to dig a little deeper into your life. A few simple questions to gently encourage you along the path of living with greater intention and clarity. These prompts are here to help you consider what's feeling good, what isn't, and what you want more or less of in the years to come.

EMBRACE

Pull out old photos, albums, diaries or journals and allow yourself to wander down memory lane. What has each decade of your life taught you so far?

_____

_____

Describe yourself in three words.

1.

_____

2.

_____

3.

_____

If your life were to be made into a film, what would the title be? And who would play you?

_____

_____

_____

Describe one of your favourite days or moments. What did it look like and how did you feel? Where were you? What were you doing? What was so special about it?

_____

_____

_____

_____

_____

_____

_____

_____

_____

When was the last time you celebrated something you achieved? How did you do this? If you can't remember the last time, how could you do it next time?

_____

_____

_____

_____

_____

_____

RESILIENCE

List 3 incidents in your life where things didn't work out and write down what you learned from these periods of adversity.

1.

   _____

2.

   _____

3.

   _____

Cast your mind back and consider the gifts and challenges that this year has brought you. What stands out the most? What really mattered?

_____

_____

_____

_____

_____

What have you learned about yourself recently. How have you surprised yourself?

1.

    _____

2.

    _____

3.

    _____

LET GO

There may be people in your life who've said or done the wrong thing or maybe it was you? Perhaps you passed judgement on someone, felt resentment or even judged yourself too harshly? Maybe you feel you let yourself down in some way? When we extend forgiveness and compassion to others we become better equipped to show it to ourselves. With this in mind...

Write down three people you could forgive or show compassion towards, in spite of their actions.

1. _____

2. _____

3. _____

Write down three things you are proud of yourself for.

1.

_____

2.

_____

3.

_____

Write three ways you could show greater kindness to yourself.

1.

_____

2.

_____

3.

_____

EVOLVE

In the months to come, which area of your life would you most like to develop? Is it related to you or your work?

What would you dream for yourself if possibilities were endless? Write down anything and everything that comes to mind. Be bold.

_____

_____

_____

_____

_____

_____

_____

_____

_____

_____

_____

_____

_____

What small things could you start to do now to slowly start shifting towards making this a reality?

_____

_____

_____

_____

_____

_____

When you think of a future without limits, do you feel sceptical? What do you think is making you feel this way?

_____

_____

_____

_____

_____

How might a well-lived life look and feel for you? Write down your version of hope below.

_____

_____

_____

_____

_____

_____

_____

_____

_____

_____

_____

_____

_____

_____

PROMISES

Without taking too long to think about your responses, complete these sentences:

In the days following...

I will make more time for...

I will nurture my spirit with...

I will learn more about...

I will be open to...

I will pay attention to…

I will embrace…

I will let go of…

I will take courage in…

I will forgive myself for…

I will start saying "yes" a little more to…

I will start saying "no" a little more to…

This time next year I will have discovered…

"My children don't need me to save them, my children need to watch me save myself."

Glennon Doyle

FURTHER READING

BOOKS

Wabi Sabi: Japanese Wisdom for a Perfectly Imperfect Life by Beth Kempton (Piatkus; 01 edition, 2018)

Big Magic: How to Live a Creative Life, and Let Go of Your Fear by Elizabeth Gilbert (Bloomsbury Publishing, 2015)

The Gifts of Imperfection by Brené Brown, (Hazelden FIRM; 1st edition, 2018)

Tiny Beautiful Things: Advice on Love and Life from Someone Who's Been There by Cheryl Strayed (Atlantic Books; Main edition, 2013)

Wild: A Journey from Lost to Found by Cheryl Strayed (Atlantic Books, 2015)

Annie Leibovitz at Work by Annie Leibovitz (Jonathan Cape, 2008)

Steal Like an Artist by Austin Kleon (Workman, 2012)

Keep Going by Austin Kleon (Workman, 2019)

When Things Fall Apart: Heart Advice for Difficult Times by Pema Chödrön (Element Books, 2007)

PODCASTS

Magic Lessons with Elizabeth Gilbert
Oprah's Super Soul Conversations
Unlocking Us with Brené Brown
Letters From a Hopeful Creative
How to Fail with Elizabeth Day
Happy Place with Fearne Cotton

NOTES

THE END OF THE BEGINNING

1. "Before Tsunami hit the Thailand land in 2004" YouTube video, https://www.youtube.com/watch?v=uYCV1MLU5Us

2. Dr. Brenda Kelly, speaking at ARC AGM, Information and Support Day, November 2019.

3. Information provided by Jane Fisher, ARC https://www.arc-uk.org/

4. *Peanuts,* created by Charles M. Schulz, 1950s onwards.

5. Mando Meleagrou, speaking at ARC AGM, Information and Support Day, November 2019.

CHAPTER 1: CREATIVE SELF-CARE

1. *The Creative Brain,* directed by Jennifer Beamish and Toby Trackman, Netflix, 2019.

2. *Floyd Norman: An Animated Life,* directed by Michael Fiore and Erik Sharkey, Michael Fiore Films, 2016.

3. Elle Wright, *Ask Me His Name* (Lagom, 2018).

4. Elizabeth Gilbert, *Big Magic: How to Live a Creative Life, and Let Go of Your Fear* (Bloomsbury Publishing, 2015).

5. Sara Novak, "Maternal Depression Is Most Common at Four Years Postpartum", *What to Expect*, January 29, 2015, https://www.whattoexpect.com/wom/toddler/0528/maternal-depression-is-most-common-at-4-years-postpartum.aspx

6. Laura Pashby aka @circleofpines on Instagram.

7. "Why Maslow's Hierarchy of Needs Matters", *The School of Life*, YouTube video, https://www.youtube.com/watch?v=L0PKWTta7lU

8. David Allen, *Getting Things Done: The Art of Stress-free Productivity* (Piatkus, 2015).

9. "Do What Ignites Your Soul", Se.1, Ep.1, *Magic Lessons with Elizabeth Gilbert* (podcast).

10. Julia Cameron, *Artist's Way for Parents, The: Raising Creative Children* (Hay House UK, 2013).

11. "Cheryl Strayed to Moms - 'Pursue Your Passions Like a MOFO", Se.1, Ep.2, *Magic Lessons with Elizabeth Gilbert* (podcast).

CHAPTER 2 : LETTING CURIOSITY LEAD

1. Clive James, as quoted in: Elizabeth Gilbert, *Big Magic: How to Live a Creative Life, and Let Go of Your Fear* (Bloomsbury Publishing, 2015).

2. "Brené Brown on 'Big Strong Magic'", Se.1, Ep.12, *Magic Lessons with Elizabeth Gilbert* (podcast).

3. "TEDxTucson : George Land The Failure Of Success", *TEDx Talks,* YouTube video, https://www.youtube.com/watch?v=ZfKMq-rYtnc

4. "Brené Brown on 'Big Strong Magic'", Se.1, Ep.12, *Magic Lessons with Elizabeth Gilbert* (podcast).

5. Elizabeth Gilbert, *Big Magic: How to Live a Creative Life, and Let Go of Your Fear* (Bloomsbury Publishing, 2015).

6. Beth Kempton, *Wabi Sabi: Japanese Wisdom for a Perfectly Imperfect Life* (Piatkus; 01 edition, 2018).

7. "Melody Ross - Grief, Loss, and the Healing Power of Art", *The Creativity Habit* (podcast).

8. Melinda Gates, *The Moment of Lift: How Empowering Women Changes the World* (Bluebird; Main Market edition, 2019).

9. "Stealing Like an Artist with Austin Kleon - Part 2" *The Futur with Chris Do* (podcast).

10. Maria Popova, "How Einstein Thought: Why "Combinatory Play" Is the Secret of Genius", *Brainpickings,* https://www.brainpickings.org/2013/08/14/how-einstein-thought-combinatorial-creativity/

11. Karen Andrews, *Being Heard* (podcast).

CHAPTER 3 : THE MINDFUL PHOTOGRAPHER

1. "Jeff Ascough Wedding Photography Masterclass", Watford, April 2009.

2. Eric Kim, "10 Things Garry Winogrand Can Teach You

About Street Photography" https://erickimphotography.com/
blog/2012/08/20/10-things-garry-winogrand-can-teach-you-
about-street-photography/

3. Ira Glass, "The Gap", produced by Daniel Sax on Vimeo
https://vimeo.com/85040589

CHAPTER 4 : WHOLEHEARTED CREATIVITY

1. "Statistics about stillbirth", *Tommy's*, https://www.tommys.
org/our-organisation/charity-research/pregnancy-statistics/
stillbirth

2. Estimated TFMR information provided by Jane Fisher, ARC:
https://www.arc-uk.org/

3. Caelainn Hogan, "Why Ireland's battle over abortion is
far from over" *The Guardian,* October 3, 2019 https://www.
theguardian.com/lifeandstyle/2019/oct/03/why-irelands-battle-
over-abortion-is-far-from-over-anti-abortionists

4. "Listening to shame | Brené Brown", *TED,* YouTube video, https://
www.youtube.com/watch?v=psN1DORYYV0&feature=emb_
title

5. "Pema Chödrön: Welcoming the Unwelcome" *Oprah's Super
Soul Conversations* (podcast).

6. Brené Brown, *The Gifts of Imperfection* (Hazelden FIRM; 1st
edition, 2018).

7. Cheryl Strayed, *Tiny Beautiful Things: Advice on Love and Life
from Someone Who's Been There* (Atlantic Books; Main edition,
2013).

8. *Back to the Future II,* directed by Robert Zemeckis, Universal

Pictures, 1989.

9. John Grant, "GMF", track 3 on *Pale Green Ghosts,* Bella Union, 2013.

10. Derrick Carpenter, MAPP, "The Science Behind Gratitude (and How It Can Change Your Life)" *Happify Daily,* https://www.happify.com/hd/the-science-behind-gratitude/

11. *They Shall Not Grow Old,* directed by Peter Jackson, WingNut Films, 2018.

12. "Cheryl Strayed to Moms- 'Pursue Your Passions Like a MOFO'", Se.1, Ep.2, *Magic Lessons with Elizabeth Gilbert* (podcast).

CHAPTER 5 : PER ASPERA AD ASTRA

1. *How to Fail with Elizabeth Day* (podcast).

2. Rob Bell, "The Joy's of Growing Younger", *Oprah's Super Soul Conversations* (podcast).

3. *Frozen,* directed by Chris Buck and Jennifer Lee, Walt Disney Pictures, 2013.

4. Martha Beck, *Thriving in Turbulent Times,* 2020.

5. David Kessler, "David Kessler and Brené on Grief and Finding Meaning", *Unlocking Us with Brené Brown* (podcast).

6. Nora McInerny, "We don't 'move on' from grief. We move forward with it", *TEDWomen,* 2018 https://www.ted.com/talks/nora_mcinerny_we_don_t_move_on_from_grief_we_move_forward_with_it?language=en

7. Eckhart Tolle, "Acceptance of Troubled Times", *Oprah's Super Soul Conversations* (podcast).

CONCLUSION

1. "Knock, Knock", S1 Ep13, Six Feet Under, HBO, 2001.

NOTES ON THE AUTHOR

Suzie Jay Goldsmith began her career as a secondary school teacher before setting up her photography business in 2009. Over the years she's photographed weddings, families and events, developing an extensive portfolio photographing luxury brands such as Jimmy Choo, Vogue, Balmain, Nicholas Oakwell and Sophia Webster.

Suzie now teaches photography to her online community and mentors other photographers to assist them in pursuing their own business goals and dreams.

Suzie lives in the UK with her partner Paul and their daughter, Jasmine.

Printed in Great Britain
by Amazon